SONGS OF SADNESS

(A Book of Poems)

Musings on Life's Tragedies

LALITHA IYER

Edited by

Dr Tapan Kumar Pradhan

Poems included in this volume are purely creative works of art based on the author's personal experiences. Unless otherwise indicated, all the names, characters, businesses, places, events and incidents mentioned in this book are either the product of the author's imagination or used in a fictitious manner. Any resemblance to actual persons, living or dead, or actual events is purely coincidental.

This book is being sold with the condition that it shall not, by way of trade or otherwise, be lent, re-sold or otherwise circulated without the prior consent of the publisher. No part of this book may be reproduced or copied in any form by any means or reproduced on any disc, tape, digital media or other information storage devices etc without the written permission of the publishers.

ISBN : 978 – 81-945797-3-1

First Paperback Edition 2020

published and marketed by
KOHINOOR BOOKS
www.kohinoorbooks.com

Kohinoor Star Publications Private Limited
2293-A, REC Road, Mancheswar Rail Station
Bhubaneswar – 751 017

CONTENT

PART-I :- Mansion of Grief

PART-II :- Seasons of Suffering

PART-III :- Betrayal in Love

PART-IV :- Born a Woman

PART-V :- Old Age Curse

PART-VI :- Prisoner of My Cell

PART-VII :- I Seek Freedom

EPILOGUE

ACKNOWLEDGEMENT

I owe a deep debt of gratitude to my fellow poet friends on Poemhunter website. My poetic craft has been shaped by the honest feedback received from thousands of readers. Although I have published my poems online on several websites, it is on poemhunter.com that I received wholehearted support from many kindred souls.

Dr Tapan Kumar Pradhan offered to present my poems in a book form. Many years ago I had requested Dr Tapan to write a few poems for me. I had also once requested him to gift a book of his choice to me. He had promised to me both. I think he has far exceeded my expectations. I have discussed with him several of my poems at length. I have also discussed with him the underlying unity among all the major religions of the world including Christianity, Hinduism and Islam. I believe that he shares my thoughts on the relevance of Christ's teachings for the modern world. I have full faith in his capacity to honestly interpret my poems.

LALITHA IYER

FOREWORD

This book contains 121 poems under seven different parts. All the poems are themed on human suffering and sadness. But the book is not pessimistic in its approach. Rather the book explores the underlying spiritual foundation of the human emotion of sadness.

Although the poems describe universal suffering, they are also largely autobiographical. The book shows the poet's journey from initial disenchantment with the selfish materialistic world to her gradual awakening to the existence and possibility of true love lurking behind the external clouds of illusion and suffering.

The largest part of the book is on Betrayal in Love. These poems indirectly represent events and experiences in the poet's personal life. According to the poet, the natural attraction between man and woman is a reflection of the universal love force immanent in all creation. Marriage of two adults through mutual consent is not only a holy sacrament, but also a divine form of worship of God in human form. True love finds fulfilment through the covenant of betrothal and marriage. Breaching of that covenant is a breach of man's eternal relationship with God. The personal pain of betrayal is graphically rendered by the poet through stark imagery.

Lalitha Iyer is a spiritual poet. Although she has written extensively on the scriptures of all major world religions, her meditations on Christ and Buddha have been most revealing and uplifting. Her knowledge of world scriptures like Vedas, Gita, Bible and Quran clearly reflects in her poetry.

Lalitha has written thousands of poems in different languages. Many of these poems are already scattered over the internet in various forms. This book is a humble attempt to bring the best amongst all those poems under a single comprehensive organised framework. I have selected these poems on the basis of their immediate relevance to the broad theme and structure of this book. These need not be the most representative of Lalitha's immense poetic oeuvre. Poems on sadness formed the bulk of Lalitha's early poetry. So this book primarily showcases Lalitha's earlier works.

In many of the poems included in this volume, the poet has provided footnotes to throw light on the conceptualisation as well as the scriptural and historical background of the theme. Occasionally I have provided additional notes to drive home the spiritual undertones of a poem. My notes essentially contain my views, and need not reflect the poet's original view on the matter.

Many of the poems have been edited by me to conform to the overall design of the book. Some poems were originally in free flowing passage form. These have been modified and tweaked slightly so as to have a more presentable verse form. I have been in close correspondence with the poet for almost a decade. I have discussed both poetic techniques as well as scriptural interpretation with the poet over hundreds of fruitful hours. So I have reason to believe that I understand the poet's point of view behind these creations. I am thankful to the poet for allowing me the liberty to freely explore and interpret these spiritual gems.

Some of the poems contained in this book have appeared in slightly different versions on various websites and online platforms. The poet has also been editing and tweaking her poems online from time to time. However, I am presenting the poems as received by me from the poet during my extensive correspondence.

In my extended online correspondence with the poet, I used to address her affectionately as "Lolita". Lalitha Iyer and I myself had jointly composed around 200 poems on the Lolita theme. I have provided snippets of those exchanges with her at certain places in the book to provide context of the poem.

EDITOR

INTRODUCTION

The present volume contains the enigmatic poet Lalitha Iyer's poems depicting human sorrow in its myriad dimensions. These include poems on betrayal in love, death, separation from loved ones, failure in endeavour, social injustice, pain of old age, loneliness and the suffering of poor destitute people due to lack of human touch in society. However, the sadness depicted in Lalitha's poetry are less about personal tragedies in the poet's life, and more about universal suffering due to unbalanced life devoid of inner spiritual understanding. The pain expressed in the poems is the poet's pain at seeing large scale human suffering.

Although these poems explore depths of sadness, Lalitha is by no means a "sad" poet. She has penned hundreds of mirthful poems on love, lust and comedies of life also. She has even written extensively on religion and social issues. But those poems are not in the purview of our present volume. Her romantic poems are being separately published under the title "Songs of Love and Lust". However, even in the present volume the discerning reader can see glimpses of her innate humour while describing human pain and sorrow.

Lalitha is a revolutionary poet with a magnificent range. She has a very unique style of poetic expression which stands her apart from other poets in contemporary world literature. This consist essentially in her unbridled freedom in the use of language. Reader can find such unconventional words and expressions like "hormoned with life", "gayless", "bleeded" and "yesternight" in her poetry. She even describes the process of sexual reproduction of an embryo with words like "spermovumed". These are her own spontaneous innovations, and do not yet appear in the English dictionary. She also often deliberately misspells word for special effect. Editing her works therefore is an immense challenge, since it is difficult to decide whether to rectify an apparent misspelling or grammatical error, or to just leave them like that!

Religious Symbolism

Some of the poems in this book have made allusions to events in the lives of spiritual greats like Jesus Christ and Gautam Buddha. Jesus in his physical human form graced this earth for a brief period of thirty three years at the beginning of the modern Christian era. The momentous impact of that one short life is still being felt in the unfolding of human civilisation. That extraordinary impact emanates from the unparalleled purity, truth and love manifested in the unblemished life of Jesus the Christ.

Gautam Buddha's earth life predates Jesus Christ by about five hundred years. He taught that attachments to desire was the primary cause of sorrow. His teachings spread throughout ancient Asia, triggering a tremendous mass awakening. However with passage of time the teachings of Jesus, Buddha and other masters have become distorted. People have forgotten to apply the teachings of great masters in their personal life. The human sorrow described in this book results from that forgetfulness.

The discerning reader can find religious symbolism in almost every poem in this volume. The poem Prayer and Satan describes the obstacles faced when one dedicates oneself to spiritual practices. Use of the word Rainbow symbolises inner spiritual awakening. Melting into Nothingness reflects the desire for enlightenment through the dissolution of one's individual ego.

Unity of All Religions

Lalitha's poems do not preach any particular faith or religion. They delve much deeper than the surface meaning of religious texts. They dwell on the universal truths contained in the Holy Gospel of Christian Bible, which is the same as that expressed through the Vedas, Gita, Quran and other world scriptures.

Boundless joy is a human soul's default nature. Due to attachment to sense organs and objects of sensory enjoyment, soul becomes forgetful of its true divine nature. All sorrow result from this forgetfulness. Spiritual journey starts with one's understanding of the primal cause of one's sorrow. Constant meditation, self purification and sacrifices help in gradual removal of the veils of ignorance from the seeker's mind.

All scriptures essentially teach the same truths regarding human suffering through sense identification and final emancipation through God realisation. Therefore Lalitha's poetry is a true melting pot of the truths taught by all religions.

Scope of the Book

The 121 poems in this volume have been arranged under seven different parts, each dealing with a different dimension of human sadness. Part-I titled "Mansion of Grief" deals with loneliness inside one's own house. This has two aspects – physical loneliness due to death or distancing of near ones, and emotional loneliness due to lack of communication at an inner spiritual level. The most representative poem in this part is "The Tomb of My Love Mansion". Another poem "No One Comes for Tea" depicts the emptiness in the protagonist's spiritual life.

Part-II is titled "Seasons of Suffering". This part contains poems depicting human emotions in the five seasons of life – Spring, Summer, Monsoon, Autumn and Winter. The poem "Silent Grief of Spring" and "A Summer Lost" are almost autobiographical, and they depict the poet's own tragedies in love life. The final few poems in this part reflect the symbolism of sun and moon in one's spiritual life.

Part-III deals with "Betrayal in Love". This is the most poignant section of the entire book. Lalitha is at her best in portraying betrayal. This results from her own personal experience of betrayal in human love. The poems "My Man of Yesteryears" and "All His Soothing Lies" speak eloquently about the bitterness of a failed relationship due to betrayal.

Part-IV is titled "Born a Woman". Here the poet describes the sufferings that a woman goes through in life on account of her gender alone. Despite all talks of equality, gender bias is deep rooted in society. Overcoming the biased perception is not easy even for a woman having a highly successful career. The poem "Who Loves My Menstruation Blood" how a woman's own body can be a stumbling block in her attempts to lead a healthy normal life.

Part-V deals with "Old Age Curse". The poem "Ageless Pain in Aching Limbs" indicates that the poet is not referring to the physical pain of old age related ailments alone. "Ageless" pain refers to the pain of separation from the Creator. Symbolically old age represents an "old soul" which has gone through many experiences through many human births, and is now pining for deliverance from the cycles of birth-rebirth through God communion.

Part-VI is titled "Prisoner of My Cell". The poems in this section show how a person becomes a victim of her own doing. "Sigh of a Fallen Leaf" depicts this utter helplessness of the woman protagonist to change her circumstance.

In the last part of the book titled "I Seek Freedom", the poet seeks deliverance from grief through self-analysis and introspection. The first poem in this section is "I Saw You on the Silent Street". As the reader will find, the poet is actually referring to her own true self when she is saying "I saw you". Sorrow can be conquered only by reconnecting with one's inner self. The poems in the section reflects the poet's growing realisation that distance from God was her real cause of grief.

The very last poem in the book "A Great Soul Passes" shows the poet's ideal in life as to how to overcome personal sorrow through inner knowledge.

The Epilogue presents revealing facts regarding the true identity of Lalitha Iyer, the poet. Most readers would find it quite shocking, to say the least. But I thought it was my duty to disclose the identity of this truly world class poet, so that people worldwide can appreciate the extraordinary range of the poet's compositions.

Literary Style

Lalitha Iyer has a very unique writing style, which is free from the constraints of traditional grammar. She constantly invents new words and expressions. Many of her expressions won't be found in any dictionary. She regularly uses the small "i" to denote herself in first person singular to underplay the role of individual ego in the creative process. Many of her poems almost look like social media posts. She frequently uses SMS and Tweet type abbreviations like u for You, r for Are, hv for Have and gn tc for Good Night, Take Care etc. In the same poem her protagonist speaks in past, present and future tenses simultaneously. She deliberately uses wrong spelling for special effect – e.g. Mangoose for Mongoose. All these features make her poems an editor's nightmare. One never knows for sure whether a particular word in her poem has an inadvertent spelling error, or whether it is deliberately misspelt.

Message for Humanity

All the poems in the book essentially depict the suffering of mankind due to separation from the Cosmic Spirit. Entangled in worldly attachment, man forgets his eternally blissful inner nature. Real joy in life can be attained by retracing one's path back to God through discrimination, devotion and ardent spiritual practices.

The suffering multitude of humanity is waiting for the Second Coming of Christ for spiritual redemption. It is believed that the second coming will not be a physical resurrection of the human body of a historical Jesus, but rather a spiritual awakening within each human being. This is the very essence of Lalitha Iyer's poetry. These poems call out to the readers to shed their limiting individual ego and to merge themselves in the eternal bliss of ever expanding God communion.

PART - I

MANSION OF GRIEF

THE DEAR DEPARTED

DEATH IS STUNNINGLY FINAL

16

Truth is naked. Truth was, is and will ever be. But we humans like to wear masks.

Whether death results
from a sudden accident
or a sustained illness,

nothing in life can prepare
us for the death of a loved one.

It always catches us unawares
when we are not really prepared.

Death is so deeply personal
and stunningly final.

Nothing can emotionally
prepare us for its arrival.

With every death,
there is a loss.

With every loss,
there will be grief
that pierce us deeply.

DESERT OF LIFE

In the desert of life
there is no lover
no hubby, no wife

A desert has no water, no trees
where can you then find shades
to guard against harsh hot breeze
the nights alone are lovely
in paradise we appear to be

Breathe along with me
I am that desert
in search of love
so lonely a commodity
like dates far up the tree
how can I taste thy love tell me
an oasis emerges
but there is no horizon
sands detour all the time

till Sun rise.

HOLLOW BRICKS

When you are not here
alone I am a hollow brick
though they use me to quick
profits and gains
I am still a hollow brick
mine is nothing
you took off everything
colour and music
current and energy
all my smiles and wines
my streaming spirit
all you took one by one
when I was a kid of one
you were my mother
as I lost you in the storm
I lost my balance and calm
when I grew to a toddling roam
my doll you was who left me groan
at my teens you were my favourite maid
sending messages daily piled
you won my heart and weakened my chart
I lost in exams and learnt life truths
you went with a man of handsome stride
I wondered unreplied why not my side
when i married and stood by bedside
then you said it is time for sleep
dawns are early, duties are life
caught in the web of puzzles
wrapped in the sheets of naps
I loved the wife of mine divine
the way she walks, the way she cooks
her smell, her smiles, her delicate lies

yet she too went to the churchyard
there to sleep and bless the orchards
when the kids woke me up
my life conditioned I girdled up
my honeys they drenched me with love innocent
I inhaled, inhaled too much that they grew pleasant
soon, now, when everyone has packed to their homes
left alone am I, a Hollow Brick.

TOMB OF MY LOVE MANSION

Oh my Lord,
your mansions are full
silky robes and
silvery touches
slim damsels
with slipping hips
and dancing breasts
and brooding thighs
your bed is always flowered
with all these angels
with tender hands
and touching hearts
their snow white bridges
and coal blacked hairs
their slyful looks
and tempting strides
their whispering hooks
that clings to your manes
oh no, I am a leper
and a roadside sweeper
my hands are dirty
and my dresses torn
thoughts are barren
and thighs painfully drawn
I am a hungry woman
and my lips are thirsty
but me born in poverty
and misery is my life
my blood is in agony
and I care for no fancies
I am harsh and ruff
and I sleep in sheds

shredded with stenches
I am all filthy
my sweat is smelling unhealthy
I smell from street ends
the scent of cabbages and mounds
puss oozes from my scars
blood my from thoughts
my eyes are full of blinds
I have a vision blurted
I have a body cursed
and arched like a cruise missile
I know no polite words
but only the language of whores
who quarrel for lesser paid wages

Now, how could you behold
Me and mine
when your world is lovely littered
with woman of fantastic wombs
and tattooed tombs.........

Note :- Expressions like "slyful looks", "harsh and ruff" and "lovely littered" are Lalitha/Hemangi's original invention. Sly is an adjective and does not require a "ful". Similarly "lovely" is an adjective and not an adverb. Ruff is supposed to indicate "rough". We have not edited or replaced such expressions with conventional ones.

STRAW NEST

To build a nest
with twigs unrest
lying here, lying there
to lay some eggs
and breed some chicks
to teach them how to click
to swing in the branches
and spy through the arches
to bathe in the poodles
all cool bathed rooms
in search of green woods
fully loaded with ripened fruits
all life did I stood
for life and livelihood
my nest my homes
one for one crow-hus
same straws yet new nest
next time I breast
sweet life, luxurious breeze
small little problems
everything within reach
friends of mine
plenty and more
we dine together
that is where we gather
we dirts eat to purify the earth
our souls divine burn the heaps holy
Yet I dream of cages untold
where parrots feed on milk and grains
mellow fruits are ripe and ready
anytime to taste without buddies.

MY CHAMBER OF DREAMS

Every night
after a day of fights
as energy tides
rise and fall
when i enter my chamber of dreams
it is too weary, i die asleep.
many a dream it creeps
into my conscious fields
merging with my magnetic seals
I enter the bed
all confused head
my days have gone
night is sweet
stars are bright
moon is a sight
yet, my thoughts are a weight
in the middle of life
amidst bleeding strife
I am begging for energy
yes, my cells are on revolt
i am dwindling like a colt
my racing sperm is killed
stirring soul is tilled
I have lost my blood
blood of my hood
oh no, blood of my hold
my inner hold of pure gold
seed of my creator's mould
suddenly i am alien to this world
i dont know where it went cold
your words are hollow
they were sweet and aglow

when i was in my hormone's blow
as age has crept
emotions are swept
i miss me, kisses not adept
my body is weightless adrift
winds of monsoons they gift
me shores or sinking drifts
every dawn born again
my living urge sapped and strained
i seek the reason for life
as i go down,
diving to touch the bottom
but my masks are boredom
blues i cant touch
bluer i never more
y live, when death is sweeter
y die when life comes again.

Note :- Use of small "I" for the first person singular, and "y" for why are typical of Lalitha/Hemangi's poetic style. We have not edited such expressions to fit into conventional spelling/grammar rules.

ALONE AND CLUELESS

Alone am I,
clueless about the way
to go ahead
no sense is working
no censors to curtail
no signals to stop me
nor guide further
I take a step and
look above
as if the Sun alone shall help me ahead
I am moving since my legs are itching
I am gaining pace since I am young and living
yet, my goals are missing my brains
I am not thinking
since thoughts are no more an inkling
I am stunned,
oh no, I am frozen
my ideas nil
my intentions had nobody to kill
I watch every one march ahead
race defeating
the weaker ones
I look behind and let go ahead
the poor crippled ones
who cant meet with the stronger ones
I wonder why should they feel bad
for nature's curse why they feel sad.

Where are the trees growing?
Up, Up, Up
Where are the roots growing?
Down, Down, Down

the branches left and right
they give no clue to which side I should go

Where are the clouds going?
they cool down into rains
and the breeze take them into lanes
they donno, they too have the wind to guide
I am a human with a heart and a brain
I think hence I cant go
stuck up between materialists and matter
Spirits and Spirit intakers
Musicians and Music
Politicians and Politics
Money and Money minded ones
Mothers and Surrogates
Fathers and Fatherless
Men and Brutes
Do I need Money
to live or to die?
Do I need Love
to mate or to hate?
Do I need life
to sleep or to wake up
Sleeping life is a waste
Waking up you are a Tragedy keepsake..........

MYSELF, ALONE

Alone am I
I was a mind
when I reached my teens
then I wondered
where is my father.
Up in the blues
as the stars shone
when the earth slept
and silence spread
then I was awake
searching for your steps
I harkened your music
when the wind blew
through the woods and land
I tasted you in every new fruit
and smelt your perfume
in every buttercup
yet My Beloved,
I wanted to see you
but alas! I could not find you
among the crowd of men
who gathered around me
wherever I went
in the form of fools
dictators and impostors
I slept; but they took me
my child of night it cried
shaking my motherhood strongly
I was sad, extremely sad
I yearned to see u
to meet you I came
to temples and churches

to synagogues and mosques
Oh! no, you were not there
empty hearted I returned
in this world of physical affinities
I alone hankered for a physical entity
All alone crazily, still I wander
in my thoughts from hills and vales
to pilgrimage centres and palaces
from low moon to high sun
wherever my sight could enter

I looked for you
I ached for you
I sang for you

But you never come.

LIKE A PARROT, ALONE

Alone
all alone
I am so sad
in my caged bed

it is raining
mating birds are flying
high up in the sky
their lovely plumes
competing with grooms

the caged bird
fed well
her calling urges
kills her days
all night hours
she sleeps in fatigue

day goes by
pecking on all sundries
but when dusk enters
and twilight flutters
when every soul on earth
longs for company and hearth
when sadness covers
all earth with darkness
when the urge to mate
kindles every born soul

the poor bird
could only wish
for greener nests

and gayer mates
it is heartening
to hear it woo
mindless parrots
flying high up
far off they flash
in the eternal blues
lovely plumed
their energies zoomed
the aching heart
it grieves and grieves
till it could call
it in full volume utters
its need for company
well hormoned
weary hearted
caged hearted men
breed caged birds
brutal people
senseless couples...

NO ONE COMES FOR TEA

Wake up, Wake up
no, my child is not in bed
he is no more with me
the blankness he left
stopped my words
in Silence I portrayed
the figure and fullness
of his presence
and the meaning
of my affection

Tea Time
but I made tea for none
when you have hours and health
and money to buy tea and sugar
but none to entertain
alone you drink
only sad memories to think
the big vacuum killer link

Hey! the child from next street
no, it's not responding
want to sit upon the swing
and go up and down and sing
but, something creeps into my limbs
and makes me weak and weary
could you tell me please
when earth is overpopulated
why can't we simply
incorporate new sons?

SOLITARY WALKER

Alone the way is far
I can't walk single
all the way ahead
my burden weighs
upon my breast
and my life stresses
my veins and bones
can you help me
O passerby?

My aged limbs sway aside
my single heart beats so fast
that I stumble each step
with its racing retreat
my faltering looks fall
upon frozen hearts
that don't shake at my greying sicks
tired am I, and fatigued
pressures and pains pinch me apart
plaguing fears haunt me day in day out
stretching days and crutching nights
cripple my thoughts

O dear passerby
could you bear my soul
for just a small second
let me lie down asleep
forever in slumber
caressed by green grass blades.

BY MYSELF, ALL ALONE

it is half past day
grey head is dawning
truths provoking
me to responses

it is the time of midday
when reality pops up hot
when life hangs in between
sunsets and sunrises

we are suddenly alone
every one of us
our hormones too
upset by absurd endings

dreams all wiped clear
the fabric of romance
tripped naked
nothing remains
but shreds of reality
bold and blurting sharp

statues of ego
waxing melting under hot facts
life is slipping, limbs are groaning
you are alone, none listens
to the secrets your mind stumbles upon

you are facing the wall
and wall is walking towards you
yet it is just for you and you only

others can't share this mystery
since they cannot see
what you see now

You are all alone
when words you speak
none could understand
when the hands you shake
spears with rushing pride
when you are stuffed
amidst the cheering crowd

when the man next to you
could not see the humour
that is eating your life
you turning into a joke
and the comedy is about to end
You know
you want so much to tell
yet none could feel
the throb of your pulse.............

COME SEE, MY SON HAS NO SKIN

They burnt my son
my only son
with kerosene
no skin to sight
just the naked knight
he asked for more
Oliver's hunger core
he asked for money
to feed his honey
and babies puny
when i went
on message sent
he was lying in a sheet
just with a piece of meat
which was his body
as it added mess
groaning loud
his pain i say pain
it was plain
could you lie
with no skin
i could only sigh
my son, my child
i am his mum
oh, could you come
and tell me the outcome
the beginning or end
of this story which sends
many stories to shame
how could I say how could
one burn another cold
no feeling, eh? no feeling

i just feel reeling
my senses suffer
i am in a thoughtless hour
how could i still wonder
at the sight of his agony
you should come with me
please lend me your arms
i can't stand this harms
no, not anymore
it sickens my core
i am so helpless
i am a mother
see my child without skin
he has been burned
with oil he is burning
touch of inners with the externals
inner softness shirking and shrinking
the bloody cruel world
and his innocent tenders
oh, oh he cries out
the skin is peeled
the outer world and inner mold
i am thoughtless dear
what to fear now
what do i hear
no human schools are here
they don't teach to be humans
only for jobs and just for sums.

LET ME SING ON MY SON'S BODY

Here lies the dead body
of my son who was done
yesterday they burnt him bad
for asking more I told you sad
today, he is no more
in a plastic sheet he was
shrieking in pain and pus
a mother, I am
a mother am I
yet, the sight I can't stand
it was a cruelty
to humanity
my son, his skin has gone
only soft mass of flesh
oh, how could I kiss you
touch you with my love
how could i feel you
and still my choking tears
yesternight, when u wailed
i wept with nothing to bail
i just sank beneath
above me your skin
like a corpse it shrouded my gloom
oh God, how could humans burn
humans and slumber in barns.

RAPED BY NAZI

I feel smoked
by my own breath
I am in the camp
Camp of Hitler's
that Nazi camp
where everybody counted
moments and only moments
anytime shots may be fired
how do lives he dared
to kill so many
all lovely kids
and dear wives
and loving husbands
and just humanity
the hope of sanity
he just killed
sanctity he raped
armies seeding sons
with no father to name
women pregnant with seeds
but only misery welled
oh! how paining it is
to think of all that
to watch the cruelty
of families butchered
burnt, poisoned and gassed
terribly sad am I
though he lives no more
this darned man
the harbinger of Dark fears
whose heart was icy
and mind too crazy

Horror in frenzy
Evil in lunacy
Errored in fantasy
Terror of cruelty

my dear Jew bloods
they as cabbages we cut
were shaved from bodies
and shoved off
treated as sausages
and sundry wastages

how many lovely dreams
he smashed
how many loving maids
he crashed
raped his country women
by enemy men
and raped other women
with his own armies
I wonder
how nature with all its beauties
could bear creature of such oddities

HE WAS NO MORE

Before he spoke his heart out
he was no more;
he flew away to lands unknown
his eyes now bear no more
the dear look that shone afore.

Before his lips could utter a syllable
lungs went numb, heart heaved unavailable;
she knelt beside to sketch the smile
the tear that moistened his cheeks awhile
Alas, he took his expressions to invisible miles.

Before she smelt that he already escaped
into a world of untouchable shapes
there he lost his sex and shine
his touch and taste and look and life
she just welled his words unspoken

she was his wife

So swift do things turn around
like magic wands gods immobilise us, unsound
we like gods sprout and sermon the poor around
and learn to unlearn the kindness
mother's milk has strewn
till death whispers, dears disappear
clueless, silent and strawn.

LOVED ONES DIED

Like the Autumn leaf
lying yonder dust
all my loved ones died

My dear mother
who sunned my blinded looks
with her love and vision
she who suckled life
and warmth into my being
and seeded life to my casing
flew with the migratory birds
fancying beauty of other worlds
without saying an apology word

I took the chubby kid
only yesterday in my lap
and patted him softly
with my life blood fed
yet today he like an alien being
stands apart from me

My handful of love and passions
I poured into my heartful of emotions
still parched are my lips full of thirst
my pot of life is empty and endless
no stones of hopes raise its level to joy.

I MAY SEE YOU NO MORE

Too little hope
of seeing you
I have no tickets
my purse is empty
when I reached the shore
your ship had sailed
the crowd did not clear
for me to see you near
I wish I could
see you just
to say my last words
words of a mother
in love
I want to tell you
that the world is dangerous
that beware of dirty men
always be honest before God
and give you a hug
and all my dearest wishes
just once,
to see you
to touch your head
with my ageing limbs
trace your outline
and remember the way you were born
a child, a boy, a youth and now
you are a man facing the world
which failed me in Understanding
and in awe and despair
I am waning

LOVED ONES IN THE SKY

Peeping
at night
into the sky
I could see
the light of the eyes
of dear ones departed
when I am really sad
and ache for them bad
I could feel
their love peel
and twinkles heal
my bleeding scar

When alone
hours of emptiness eat me up
when truths stagger me
with unexpected deaths
when babies of love
my dearest ones
fall dead one by one
and truth is slapped
upon my face
when from my kneeling down
I am forced to stand up and scowl
when the tides of life
turn and move ahead
looking above the skies

I could hear them whisper
the loved ones in the stars
I sleep into my sorrows
digging sweet burrows

into their mesmerising clouds
they permit me to climb up
and sit upon their radiant laps
offering soft caresses
with their cosmic licks

At times I lie to myself
that they are there
my loved ones dead
that they send me rains
when I am parched dry
they send me rays
when I shiver in cold
that they kiss me with gale
when I yearn
for some soothening shade.

PART – II

SEASONS OF SUFFERING
FIVE SEASONS OF GRIEF

God knows the thoughts of our hearts before they land on our tongues. One who tunes into God knows the thoughts welling up in all human hearts. One who loves God knows how to talk to God in silence.

For wherever life is, there is talking. Talking is a beauty of life link, of being in existence. Talk of feelings, talk of emotions, talk of not only words but heavenly responses to nature, wind, breeze, ocean, sky, birds and all. In silence body talks, in darkness inner light talks. At night the nocturnals talk. In peace hearts talk with love. In harmony music talks with symphonies. Talking without words is the most beautiful talking. Talking with dance, talking with lyrics, talking with memories, nostalgic. When you are old and alone, you will talk to photos of dead ones, to tombs of dead ones, to your beloved ones gone by. You talk to your own feelings, you talk to them who are in your consciousness. Talking is as enormous as your silent gifts of love.

Talk to God. Talk with your heart absorbed in God. Listen incessantly to God's silent talk. Do not underestimate the power of the Word. And do not forget that the pen is mightier than all the injustices that holy earth can contain. Writing is a source of personal soul-searching to find the meaning of life on earth.

THE FOUR SEASONS

it is summer,
today sun is early
budding life freely
everyone is on the streets
lanes are full of buzzling beats
dashing life crossing the roads
lusty nature awakens early
every being bursting ripe
the breakfast hours preponed
kids of chirpy life bell
every new warmth and smell.

now it rains
it pains, in chains
mind is clogged
revolts dogged
sun never dawns
inside your thoughts
drink as you may
yet lulling moods play
as the mornings sleep
the body wheels peep
to come out or not
from the garage they plot
rainy hours kills the urge
to dress and venture out
they ask us to lie down
upon the bed and stick out
remotes act, screens accelerate
story books fly fast
hungry mouths gulp to last

Come autumn
all desire is gone
like empty blue sky
the emptiness of life
stares at your face
from computer screens

Winter and frost kills me full
I watch my grave built
by hours and seconds
freezing bites cross the line
and I feel the fill
of new born gale
winter blues stretch my gloom
i am sad and i dont bloom
purest season
cruelest in fashion
lazy bones they ache in pain
backaches multiply
and bitter moments cry

Winter makes me nostalgic
i weep for my dead ones
and sob for the broken hearts
for the shivering poor
I pray and play not
just put my thoughts into the hole
that leads to the centre of the whole
the entire season it balls up into one roll
life hanging between death and drolls.

A SUMMER LOST

The Summer is on
hot and dry;
Tortoise in the pond
it is forced to land.

the beauty of the being
roofed inside the shell
what a poetic lethargy
what a patient synergy.

the mid day is on
life has past its half run
the poor soul has no idea
what is out of its imprisoned sea

Watch the beauty
personification of serenity
heads and limbs
imageries of human senses five
perseverance they name is tortoise
poise and poetry, patient and wise
yet, roasted in the fire
oh my dear, lost is all inspires.

SILENT GRIEF OF SPRING

The day was born
but dusk came soon
take me in your arms
put me asleep with songs
a petal of softness
pressed into another
let us boom together
to form the love of garden
the colours of marvel
hugged into kisses
to form the Rainbow
dashing across the wet sky
grass blades conspired
to win the love of Spring
and breeded kids plenty
and formed the bed splendid
the furs united to form the flight
up they went the birds of delight
water drops to clouds of milk
and sailing drops to Ocean ships
Some grief has swept my heart so badly
is that your heart's missing language
words spelt from hearts
join together to musical carts
when Silent are the replies
and stubborn are the ears
messages unsent
the life heart is spent

Something, somewhere, somehow whispers
but there is now a more deeper string
between our hearts of unknown springs.

MONSOON MUSINGS

Monsoon sailed in
life is all wet;
tear clouds
and needles of rain
pour

Needling rain
injects pain
pain is beautiful
it makes life
colourful

pain is always pain
if something is sure, it is.
may be yours, may be not
but death and farewells thrive
and dear ones die
and you cry

Rain is life, life is raining
full of insecure abnormalities
between two laughters
creeps in reality
like the films that drool you
between cool ads

I can see future's silhouette
I can read your mind as far as I can mine
I read yours only in my own language
A deer cannot read
a tiger's language too.

I stand before the needles of rain
they like straight lines are drawn
between earth and sky
my heart and divine
slides of past run by
they seem to see me and whisper
I stand numb and frozen
could they see me I am triggered.

Can the unborn see us, can the dead ones watch us
Can the non-living talk and can the living non talk
Can minds talk with each other
Can talks be simply country wastes
Can my emotions be spirits of dead or unborn
Can my passions be their feelings unsown
Are we born out of dead men's balances
Are we just recycled from the remnants of dead ones
Are we only here to finish the original cycle
Are all the desires and wills Creator's own will
Come let us think together
if you could put your mind to mill
Are we just ending scenes
acted by the artists
who departed before bell?

RAIN MAKES HEART SADDER STILL

Listen to the falling of rain
Observe their dance of death
on the leaves of trees

Trees in monsoon rains
absorb and suffer
the grief of sullen skies

Watch the falling of rain
observe their mystery
Working through raindrops
on your sad heart

See how dry earth
absorbs the rain,
how life crawls out
of dead dry dust
to suffer in floods
and die again

Look at the sad leaves
darkened dark in rain
their stems shaking
young little sprouts
struggling to stand
in the monsoon drizzle

Come take a glimpse
glance at the sickening sky
from where the rain comes,
and where it goes

Follow the raindrops
with the moist eyes
of your sad heart
think of their origin
and their destination
in your silent hours

Look at the raindrops
falling on dry ground
on the barks of trees
and on the roofing tiles

Observe how the rains
make your aching heart

sadder still.

RAIN DROPS OF SEMEN

like a drop of rain
for the parched brain
the idea came flashing
and downpoured dashing
the seed of the tree
stored the brain
yet none could see
the tree and trunk inside
silence, the poetry of silence
to some it is the world
and to some it is the word
some feel it through music
and you feel it by my basics
how fragrant the first drop is
smell of semen sprouting from earth
as if earth suddenly rejoiced
hormoned with life, rained to thirst
to quench the hunger of millions
there came the drop of rain
pure drop, immaculately clear
with no germs and dust
life was drizzling in plain and pure
the first drop of fertility
from the breasts of heavens
the milk of motherhood
brims over in fullness
as monsoon baby cries
over spilt half bosoms
that liquidly suckle
the famished soil
fluid motion of life in coil.

A drop of rain
in lusty curve
a bubble of round
exciting all around
appealing the speaking
and things not speaking
expressions of nature
birds sing
babes dance
to wing, to swing
in ringing tones
all cling to hold
the gems of household
in drops of rain

LAST AUTUMN LEAVES

Look,
autumn leaves are falling
like wretched love stories
into dustbin of memories

Beauty of life falls
Into purity of death
Autumn's blue sky
Reflects the deadness
Of my empty heart

My life is like
An autumn leaf
Dry and yellow
Devoid of a story
Worthy of love

Desires fall one by one
Like the last leaves
Of my autumn silence
Battered by life.

AUTUMN OF SADNESS

A year has passed
In the barks of trees
Seasons have added
Another layer of rings
My life has no seasons
My finger has no rings
Autumn now lingers on
in memories of leaves

I was long dead
On my nuptial bed
Before autumn came
My body had a shroud
Wrapped in grief

There is no pain left
In my aching limbs
To write on dead leaves
I do not require now
Autumn's old leaves

Until next autumn
Why should we wait
Come make love
To my corpse now
Wrapped in leaves.

SOLITARY SOUL OF WINTER PINES

Shivering in winter
stark naked
sans leaves
is my solitary soul

what aches it?
pained to soul
the skin you see
just grieving white cold

winter needles in
I am alone, I am alone
God is hybernating
ghosts are wandering

give me a candle flame
just to feel the hot glow
give me a bird's chirp
just to feel the sweet lips

in this piny world of cruelties
shivers my heart afraid of future
I am in fear of losing the beauty
of life and creation's nameless agony

I am afraid and they ask me why
I am anxious, they ask me for whom
killing loneliness crawls my inside
they say these worms are bad dreams

tell me how can I kill such a bad dream
what do I spray on my loneliness to numb
but inside me still that crawling feeling
of a baby scratching walls of my womb

every second zoomed to hours
shows minutes of my sufferings
my utter helplessness booms
in the emptiness of my trappings

I cannot escape the terror of being
ghost of myself in my own womb
I wish I could sleep and escape
my dead soul's lonely wanderings.

CAGED BIRD IN WINTER OF LIFE

It was day one
the bird was swollen
with life and passion
it bluntly beat its breast
against the bars of the chest
caring least whether it hurt
or bled or pained its softs

It was day two
it twittered and tweeted
but no passerby turned
its breast swollen with bruise
now hurt alive, no more bar wars
it sang aloud to keep it alive
hear me, hear me, my agonies aloud

Days and weeks past by
poor bird now rested all day
and woke up at nights
to watch dew drops whiten the ground
night birds came and sat near the cage
wondered at a day bird lying awake like a sage
moon peeped in, cool and calm, kissing its plumage

thus life's youth past
it could watch the squirrels mate and chat
kingfishers breed and mate high in the air
storks and swans land near the water pond
woodpeckers dance, doves peck
at each other's willing neck
even moths and butterflies lived in pair
the poor bird just wept and struggled.

Pain shot up, separation killed,
but no song, no bar wars
no sighs, and no hopes
slowly it learnt it should die now
it was time to learn life should end now
or slowly death shall inch her to rest
its shot up live and watched around
to find how beautiful birds kill them unfound.

WINTER WRINKLES

Winter's feet are full of cracks
bleeding she labours without breaks

she harbours pain and undue strains
she wombs in groans and aches;
what seasons shall sprout in Springs
With a wounded smile she asks

her wrinkles are her worries for Spring's seeds
her silence is full of apprehensive eloquence
her foggy physique veils from aliens
her babies destined to bloom
are waiting for coloured seasons

Barren and childless
stuttering and shivering with chillness
ugly and alone, dark and distant
she simple and unproductive,
her beauty wrapped up deep within
for apparent onlookers she an unwanted urchin

the feet of Winter fests with parched hearts
her gloomy looks and graceless nights
killing wishes her numbed passions
she cuts icing life frozen cold.

FROZEN HEART OF WINTER

The Winter's heart was frozen thorn
every touch pricked with horns
painted memories pained on and on
there was no warmth in the misty morn

The early morn did not sing
Singing birds were sleepy wings
Dusky hours breathed not love
All life was hungry aching cowed

Grass blades stiff, the leaves stern
the greens did not smile
the blues did not beam
No sun, no hot airs, no hugs, no kisses.

The beats of music sick and lone,
laughter and mirth have slept ill born
brutal lungs bark with no singing larks
Every nest is egg-less and empty barks.

THORNED MOON

Wounded moon
it veils in half
her silvery looks
scarred by black sorrows

little by little
the night air kettles
some glow worms to her right
and smoothens her melancholic bright

the bud of beauty burst open
her red eyes full of grief
her golden bee had flown past
as she slept in the dreamy casts

life is hurt bleeds the thorn
rose is hurt blurts the morn
sea shells hurt bursts open
me myself sit by the shore
moaning undone.

MOON LIGHT MEMORIES

Sweet and sad
moon light always beads
the lace with memory leads

in my teens
my hormones oozed out
as I curled out
in the moon lit night

as I grew up
my dreams and loves
all blazed in the cool moon
my spring blood boiled
blushed with delight

all the fantasies
all the sweetest memories
romantic webs knit across
the full moon sky freckled
with millions stars

the nights were awake
when she peeped inside
I loved her in watery beds
her silvery threads woven
in warm filmy shades

yet, she weighed upon my nights
when my mother breathed that night
just that night and no more right
as she blazed at distant sight

I waited till midnight
to relieve motherless plight
at the courtyard bereft
of lovely mother's gait.

the shroud of moon light
now fell upon me tight
it choked me breathless
freezing attractions gayless

I still wonder at full moon nights
if my mother did come out of the grave
and did she engrave her love upon the pave
did the wintry dews make her shiver
and did she cry and groan in fever

the icy night evoked further
terrible sights of dead ones dear
Still, I could not bury the delicate mother
banishing the memories of full moon weather.

WAITING FOR SUN AND MOON

All day
the bird waited for the sun
the sun did not come
the bird did not sing

All night
the bird waited for the moon
the moon did not come
the bird did not sleep

It was a sad day and sad night
the poor bird had nobody to sight
it sighed day in and day out
and heaved with sighs of bleeding heart

why do we live
the bird asked
why do I sing
the bird asked

If i have no friend
nor companion
no sun nor moon either
I should die like a dew

just melt away unknown she said
next morning before the sun was up
and it did too
the bird broke herself against a thorn

that night the moon rays silvery white
stroked the sikly furs lying dead

they were too soft that the breeze touched them dear
but the bird was broken and lay dead uncared.

Poor bird, when it was aching and waiting
no one came, not even a mate of love
or a match to woes or a friendly hopper
it bleeded and fled to free itself of heart's chopper.

My days are wasted upon a love or two
My heart sighs and heaves for a dear or two
but why do I exist, without any cause
My dear bird, wish I had courage of your choice.

AFTER SUNSET NIGHT CURVES IN

When the sun sets
leaving darkness
as message
hopes sink
when it rains too
as the evening closes
you take to drinks
as something kills you
why does the night
reminds me every day
that life is dusk
and dawn is to pass
if dawn could pass
y dusk linger on
why sorrows weigh more
and joys settle less
why trust is less
and fear is growing more
When the Sun sets
blinding the sight
truths are lost
and hearts are broken
Nights curve in
with sleeps and lusts
yet, darkness to rest
mind filled with unrest.

CYCLE OF LIFE

Moon is gone
but moonlight
still shining silver
in the night

youth is gone
but painted in the air
pictures appear fair

tears are errors
mistakes of lesser understanding
fears are faithless mortals

life is a cycle
meetings are mere miracles
memories are pages revisited

identity is a false certificate
into thin air ends up the life
into one nothingness we go up

truth is beautiful
all beautiful things are ugly
when bared naked
they are not sweet nor smiling

life is a lesson
ageing is the teacher
pains of physique are beatings
for forgetting home works
pains of heart are poor grades
in the exams where concentration fails

where no infinite parallels meet
everything is fine when meeting is not cheating
meeting to meet again
parting to part again
then meet we part
part we meet
life is going on and on
we are nothing

but dots of semi-gods.....

PART – III

BETRAYAL IN LOVE

WOMAN AND THE LESSER HALF

LOVE ALONE

The whole life is a search for a little bit of love. If we do not get it, we become psychologically and physically ill. If we experience it, then there is Rhythm in our souls and we dance in those rhythms...

All the moments in which you do not love, are wasted moments of life which will never come back. Our call is to love. There is no meaning in life without love.

Love and love alone can bring you into the world of beauty. Your soul is in need of love. The deepest longing in you is love. Love is spiritual nourishment.

Love is God's hands and arms. He hugs his beings through love. When we are pure in mind, or when there is no mind, God puts his hand made of divine energy through our hearts. Through us that hand goes to the heart of our beloved. Now who are you, and who am I, to stop, start, punctuate, and intervene that love?

MY MAN OF YESTERYEARS

Once I missed a man
in my teens
he was my greens
so fresh a youth he was
and flaming rage it was
he stood touching the sky
and tough as wood of wild
life was pouring from him
as if the air would sink me deep
the age was that of mirages
every pit was oozing with oceans
every stone was sparkling gem
air was full of kisses
heart filled with wishes
he looked down at me
and there I melted a candle
the sound of steps he took
send currents of electric tricks
that was what a loss
I thought, when his wife I cost
but, now when as age creeps on
when the air of films flimsy
rained by life truths messy
cleared up, I say, cleared up
when no hormonal disorders
twinkle the looks and twists the hips
as moon does not kill you
and earth does not hug you
any man is just a sperm injector
Creator's machine for pollination
only source of human multiplication
attached with the necessary tools

and of the accessories of contrivance
detached to the single handed motivation
to seed and seed anyway and every which way
just to finish the one and only operation
the presence of him was just nothing
not just nothing, but he makes me hate
hate what life is, what my body is to me
and abhor that beast in his heart
but for the beast, a man is not whole
and but for the man, the beast is dead
man and the beast like a coin of lust
reverse the coin and there he is
he the tailed head or the headed tail
everywhere he issues, unlicensed
his survival depends on his sperms
his identity marked by count of germs
he picks up and sprays into gutter

now that that part of my life is over
I find everything is just a cover
a cover to just litter
just to litter, sir, litter
in the stinking human gutter
and our youth is such a joke
to poke is a joke
and joke is that poke

yet, now when everything is clear
what the hell am I doing here
I miss me, my man
no more am I a woman
for that man in me
I have kicked down
I will woo no more man

Never, never a man again
this is an insult to creativity
yet here I am, pupiling myself
say, why dress young women
if not for lying to themselves
why lying if no child is coming
why child if too many is too sad
why do young women dashingly dress
if not for the lure of gutter's stink
are they all the prostitutes fresh
all the lasses from twelve to thirty
the budding blooms to be fooled
by creator's mysterious man rod
all sensuality and romantic verses
divinity succumbing to satanic curses.

Note :- This poem has autobiographical undertones and overtones. Hemangi Sharma as Lalitha Iyer had disclosed to me details of her past life incidents. Her self-discovery was the result of her life long struggle to overcome the betrayal by a man she had loved in previous life.

Single Handed Motivation :- Instead of single-minded, the poet has used the expression "single handed" to make the act mechanical and impersonal – i.e. devoid of mindfulness that is associated with true love.

SECRET THAT STINGS

I wished
to tell you
the secret that stings
deep within
my heart's strings

yet I thought
time was unripe
and kept it hooded
beneath my pipe
all precious and prized

yet, when i got up this dawn
I whispered it all aloud
to wake you up
from your dry dreams
your cold ears held it not
they tanked not the words
I was late, too late

I blanked out unread.

HELPLESS NEXT DOOR

You are next door
I could even knock
but when I stand up
my throbs mock
and I sit helpless....

I wonder
what have you worn today
blued, whitened or limed you are
wonder what moods you share
what must me in your thoughts
you are just next door
yet, I am afraid to knock......

It is a fool's errand
I just sit and watch
you could hear me
if I call, just whisper
you could see me
if only I could
wave my hand
I fear
lest i lose my control
I sit
and wonder
and surrender
to my impotent wishes.........

ALL HIS SOOTHING LIES

I talk to him
hanging at the wall
alone, when all life sleeps
I look into his eyes
and ask
in Silence
he understands
no words
neither voices he needs
I peep into
he says you are pretty
just to make me happy
I tilt my face
and he fondles with love
and pats my back
comforting my loss
as my tears
trace the history
he teases me
with tempting jokes
I look sheepishly
in to my own mirror
and sleep into
the soothing lies.

Note :- Autobiographical ruminations

LANGUAGE OF LOVE

you write it
it is too silly
the words are silky
when you spell them
too smooth and shelled
when you speak them out
you are a fool
when you think of it
you feel ashamed
and when you see some
with blushes on face
and fancy dresses
and mad rushes
you know she is stupid
yes, the script unwritten
the sentence half broken
feelings galore
yet, fails at a single stroke
it is all folly
yet, something overwhelms
you are the master
yet somehow you are a slave
you say no
yet you say yes
the more you deny
the more you admit
the globe of emotions
the oceans of musings
the seas of buts
the canyons of inhibited passions
the language of love is silence
darkness covers

the acts of love
but, yet, the mirror shames
the images kill you
they tease your aims
when you sing aloud
you know all are hearing
when you write in verse
you know they will chase
these peeping Toms
to plunder and exploit your space
yesterdays are dead
tomorrows are dead
indeed
this moment
it torments
yesterday you failed
tomorrow you are exiled
yet, today it asks you
make a book of me
sing for me a song
of my unsung portions
trace a sketch of my fig
they will never have to dig
and now how to marvel
your codes to decipher
you washed me ashore
in the golden sands
i am yet to recover
nothing is clear
only a couple of blues
sea waves they curl
upon my hazy looks
still i am stuck
can you hear the bells

distant temple yells
the moon and stars
they winked upon
twinkling their eyes
as if everything is a lie
and still I am tested
I have to muster
strengths to master
language which is not foreign
yet, I cannot tell her

that 'I love you Gin'

THE VULGAR MAN

so cheap he was
he was stinking
with inner evil
his smoking lungs
smoldered on
with crap ness

in his sweet words
the foulest stench
of inner wickedness
is coded deep
and his looks speak
of things his mouth
will never leak

but all was well
the drama he was playing
was of his own will
splendid was the going
and he too felt
the tricks he had mastered
and the world fooled by monsters

yet, will of the Creator
and Vision of the Divine
was waiting upon him
and dramatic shows just began
his loved ones were shut up
and bundled to bottomless tubs
his life force dried up
his black eyes opened up

soon the hurt holed him up
and his vulgar views
cursed him shut up

he learnt that life is
more than you decipher
there is more to learn
the more you infer
you can lie to others
but you only lie to yourself
and as your lies hoard up
your life missions coils to shelf.

SWEET PASTRY OF TRAGEDY

Flavourless
she tasted the pastry
and said
little she knew
the love that mixed
and sweetened the affection.

Shells and pearls
childhood and innocence
shells combine with;
to flavias,
pearls
of costly shops
glitter more;
sadly spoken

Eating him
I wonder
how ugly it is
quipped she;
while beauty of eating
lies in absorption of love
and lovely emotions
and sweet feelings

Dear Flavia
A Tragedy
in thy Name
I found....

PREGNANT WITH YOUR CHILD

When we met
in the sunset
i saw the step
of identical lefts
and my legs i fit
and i was right
legs into legs
and arms into arms
yes, it was a proper fit
hand and hands
hair to feet all stood
equally understood
the sun has gone
the shadows no more
it is dark
between moon and the stars
some time to hide
hide the burning tide
to stand on my feet
loosening your hugging feet
i shook aside
you and all yours
just to lie alone
and find my home
to cleanse my hands
and free my land
from the Ocean
to the air of mission
no more confusions
day is over
wisdom only a cover
to do or not to do

the things which we decide
to do or not to do
yet, you touched
yes, you touched me
not with a hand
or a lip or a stick
with a child of mine
inside your womb
you touched me
with my own life
deep within you
the flesh and blood of mine
the softest seed of my hope
my faith in life
it is with that child of mine
which did u steal?
no, you not of that kind
may be we know behind
before, ages past
may be we shared the start
heart to heart before depart
may be that was my gift chart
to trace you out as we separated
from our home to deserts isolated.

MY SECRET FLAME

I can hear
when you are near
what you think
written without ink
then you sing
and my lips too bring
the words into fresh ring
do you understand
i am at edge of a band

I can feel your words
they speak to me in roads
lined in queue they hoard
to destinations aboard
the drum you beat
roars in my heart
the twinkle in your looks
ripple through my books
could you feel my pulse
on your impulse.

It is a secret
is it a secret
all minds could
if they imprint
upon my paint
some of their heart steps
and even missteps
I am too confused
the cement is always wet
and no mansion is ever set

Day by Day
the ripples do die
for I am dissolved
my solvent is in hide
again the tide washes out
leaving me all drained and dry
Life is ebbing, candle is short
wind is blowing, my flame tapers
bye-bye to my trespassers
cruel immigrants all
haunting cursers.

LIFE HURTS

Hurting my life
death comes
every beauty
it kills untidy

I dress up
colourful and gay
just the thought of the day
kills every singing spray

when I pen I do frown
my name is nothing
my reading is failing

after years of travel
you reach at the marvel
that journey teaches you the art
of landing upon at the very start

if it is not the distance
travelling teaches you wisdom
of living a life without rum
just to exist and vanish to mum

they are not my roses
seeded by my hands though
they are not my lines
from somebody's book copied crimes...

PETALS SANG MUSIC OF DEATH

The petal said
I miss my dear colour
the lovely coat of red
that it yesterday had
has faded today
into yellowish bred
I loved the colour
it hugged me a lover
now, it is gone
gone is gone, dead is dead
i am on the street
trampled by dust and heat

the leaves loved their green
little did they know
that the green will fade away
green and leaf inseparable
they were born together
like eyes and sight
but age and fate
decided who go with who
soon a day of storm
took away the pride of the calm
and swept by the hands of morn
leaves lost their hoods in shame
lost is lost; cost of life it's gone.

the sandy beaches too mused
silent waves are singing loud
for them to hear, to rejoice
blue skies hummed in response
it is to kiss the heavens they dance

yet, when the last quake tremored
and waves zoomed into large demons
and hell came into earth licking all
did they sing, music was dead
yes, music of death it's voiced every bed.

HUNTER'S ARROW

It is time to go
but you did not tell me
I came all the way
just to share mine all day
yet, you have gone
i am sad
it was so bad
a life's creation to mad
when the baby asks
where is my daddy
when she under sun basks
reminding of your walks
what to tell
when did the bell toll
life does not returns back
time gone is time packed
I love the sparrows
now they don't nest here
they worry about tomorrows
when hunters kill with arrows
death they learn from past
history teaches beasts fast
humans, we forget, we fools
dead are you, so what
you are in me- I caught
you with my little heart
when me babe you did
taught the world in pots
as the ants lined
as we crossed them signed
when the smell of rains
soaked our soil with sprains

as the clouds moved
them with speed we viewed
the first dive into the water
fear and urge in totter

Look, my home is lost
when he flew he took it too
my cares unwanted
my smiles untreated
i am barren without bulbs
the glowing bulbs of life
you took my current
now my mind is in a torrent
i am upset
my trends reset
yet i forget
i start to love just
a new comer in my list.

BROKEN BRANCH OF LOVE

It hung there
half alive, half dead
clinging to the ever green trunk
the bleeding branch inaudibly struck

it can see, but not speak
it has feelings, but it won't express
it can hear, but cannot react
it wants to tell but was dying inch by inch

the half open eyes gemmed half dead looks
truth glistened upon the dying sight
it was a moment of wisdom dawned upon
from reality's hands, treasured so long.

PRICK IN THE PETAL

So soft the petal is
who pricked its breast?
so saintly a chest
reaped with lovely harvest
the dust settles
on its lovely bed
and hurts it red
rubbing with it hard
some hearts are
softer than the smooths
of silky woven cloths
hurt are their tenders
when a word a hunter
renders
I can feel the pain
as if it rains
in an alien train
a stranger remote
with no wise coat
cut by my words
and left my sailing hoard.

PAINFUL HORMONES OF MY LOVE BED

The child
at the feet of mother
figures her toes
and licks her legs
and finds solace
climbing up the way
and sleeps with love
embraced in the lap
the milk of life
is brimming in the breasts
and milk of heart
is streaming in the looks
oh, what a sight
to see the innocent kid
surrender at the mother of wombs.

At bed, at nights of love
when the lovely maiden
unveils her naked emotions
and shares her feminine wishes
of beauty and eloquence
and creeps into the land of a man
and sleeps in peace surrendering all
the body underneath
and blossoming life in her forms
faith of life and future born
the night is born, a true knight at birth.

When by pain and misery
your limbs ache
and dreams are over
and dramas are finished

now, at an age
when hormones don't function
and harbours don't ships berth
when body's nakedness irks
as the skin shrinks
and face wrinkles
and all tales of teens
turn into wasted frames
age when emotions solidify
and equations merge softly
when the inner aches
surface and charge you with shakes
in a crowd you are an unwanted make
then, as you lift hands above
and pray with heart felt gloom
there when the tears roll down
and simple life teaches smiles
the Surrender is sorrowful
yet beautifully mould.

THORN OF MY LIFE

No I am not blaming the thorn
the rose needed it..
when a bud
to protect from plucking hands
when blossomed
safe from suckling bands
the rose slept
while the thorn crept
wildly adept
upon the petalling fingers
when the rose aged
and sees no reason
for the thorn's missions
now the rose
ready to free
from the plant
and adorn the world
hates the thorn
that accompanies it.

TOUCH ME NOT

Touch me not
in my depths
for they are skies
that go on and on
and you may not reach
my inner recess stretch
the journey to the heavens
is a going of no ends
its the being
not the ending
but the beginning
is the living
there is no goal
and if you intend
then you fail
no missions to achieve
it is only the slow perceives
the dawn begins at night
every fragment little by little
develops at the darkness
with the aid of stars and moons
morn is born at midnight
that is why they say it right
touch me not, i am thine
your bare touch is a waste
it is a sign of senseless ache
when i am not in my body
but in yours
why touch me then
and reason forsake.

WHEN ALL DREAMS WERE LOST

I am done;
my woman hip
deep dipped
in the sticky mud
stench of marsh
struggles me
for want of breath

I have never thought of
never ever dreamt of
those pricking thorns of life
life could be made of stubborn walls
walls made of scornful cements
my lazy mind could not fathom
where good babies are born
and where bad babies are born
In my childhood I learnt
that all babies are innocent
that seeds make the tree
but then what happens in between
I messed up myself
before I could retreat
wave after wave
made my shores dirty with wastes
I knew not the art of swim
yet, I beat my chest
and started to stick
I was beaten
every new idea battled my impressions with
I was born free; brought up free; I knew no chains;
my flow was not arrested till I met life

life I only dreamt of
when I was in my schools
Colleges caressed my dreams
and added colour and richness
I was wild with passion
fuelled by nature's sanctions
the blue sky blissed me
the brown earth sprouted my lusts
I smelled in the birds flight
my free desires, let loose high
every leaf kissed my interiors
I quivered with every vibrant life
the day I met life
he was standing behind the wall
that I thought was magic with a ball
I slipped down
hapless, unarmed, suddenly I fell
that I could never reequip
staggering no, sucked by the messy corridors
pulled by multi-dimensional questions
who, what, where, why, how,
I lost my sight,
my senses failed
who is my friend?
who is my love?
who wants to kill me?
who is what and how and why?
I lost my sanity,
I became eccentric
I started slipped like Alice
I met with strange fashioned men and women
I could not fathom evil as evil was lethal to think of
I was afraid I too shall become evil lot
I watched beauty rise from the grass

and there spotted mongooses and squirrels
I can't tell what did I suffer
for it was not physical at all
body I trained for all emergency lots
she never ditched me
she was disciplined and honest too
hungry, she smiled, feasted she smiled,
but the world of heart and mind,
it was tossed by battles of confusions
and I was sinking till my hips were lost
At last as I resigned, statued to my fate
I could see not everything was lost
life was just a dream, I woke up
oh the hands of God, they stroked me within
I lay upon the stench, unaware of its wretched stock
flavoured by richness of wisdom of the learned cake
I laugh now, my ringing echo, like rippling waters.

SCARS WHICH NEVER HEAL

It never heals
the scar of red
every dusk
it reappears
like the phoenix
from the ashes of burning sun.

Memories never die
they are topped
by new
like the game of kids
one upon another
impregnant with haunting kills
remember not we the happy hours
but the burns they sing aloud
deeper they pain, longer they flame.

Remember the first insults
still, day afresh
the first beating to confidence
to self expression
and urge to show off teen images
the first upon the soft feathery passion
crushing and crumbling the furred lovely mansion
scars, scars, scars,
no bars, every being wretched and desperate
bruised ye learn brutality's strength

broken hearted
what a beautiful word
yet heart never breaks
only desires char

the lovely buds wither
childish fantasies tombs bear
every little baby
on its way to granny
asserts its rightful beauty
bubbles of dreams
dreaming bubbles
kisses of hopes
hoping kisses
melting half way ice creamy
grey hairs thus wisdom wavy.

Scar of red thus dusk carry
every night clothes the shroud of sky
with hands of darkness, sobbing and sighing
yet through the holes in the rags of misery
stars whisper, twinkle twinkle
moon smiles jingle jingle
every failure every beauty toes
you learn to sky and earth hug in rues.

HOUR OF BETRAYAL

I almost knew it coming
Writing was on the wall
And whole world knew
I too was warned, warned
Warned, I was warned
But I strangely trusted
Trusted, trusted, trusted
The goodness of man
I trusted, I trusted
and got betrayed

I lived my dream
I died my dream
It was a dream only
From which I awoke
But one day too late

When it came
Sky went dark
And from that dark
It came like a knife
Piercing my heart
Into two halves :
The ugly one
The dead one

He is gone now
I do not shed now
Those tears of grief
Flame of my old heart
Is consigned to history

THE RACE I LOST

I am sitting
still in the starting
no, I did not run
it was not a fun
I knew, yes I knew
there is nothing new
that I can't compete
my limbs won't treat
my racing as neat
my brains won't beat
wasted with silly feats
I am still sitting at the start.

they all raced
red hot faced
all mad with joy
of pushing aside boys
jumping upon the tracks
that others laboured to mark
trampling with shoes
upon clueless bared toes
I am sad,
not for me
but for the losers
i did not lose
see, i did not join in the race
but for those who bled
and suffered in the shed
lost their lives
parted with their wives
gave up all dimes
just to win the prize

oh, the prize coveted
for the sake of a medal
and all this trumpets
their sound inciting the rest
in a medal, a hollow medal
many a dear loved ones seal
their fate, to stupid exiles
I wait, sobbing
yet, I wait too innocent was I
I want to run now
its time for next row
once i have seen the race
now i dont mind the chase
nor do i dash in craze
i have grown-up
i am no more for the end
i have fun with the going
yes, the end is always boring
it is all finished
win or lose, it is over
the drama is no more
the stage is snoring
now again for a match
am I a match
I am not ready
but who asks me buddy
I am goaded by unknown hands
by winds unseens i am sanded
yes, the race is no more on the ground
it is going on the underground
in the future
it is not my nature
yet, i have to go
no, i can't say no, no

they all are racing
and they all drowned in the in thing
my turn, i have to
behind me, oh, the sluggish ones
they are trotting from my backs
i cant speak, silence is telling
it is spelling my destiny
did i lose, do you think
that i have lost the thing
ha, ha, its a joke
a funny joke
humour in uniform
or uninformed....

PART – IV

BORN A WOMAN
VICTIM OF OWN GENDER

THE TWO HALVES OF GOD

Two is joy. In creation everything is created in only two. Even the sprouting bud comes in twos. Sun and moon, day and night, two ears, two nostrils, two eyes, two cheers, two legs, two hands, two lungs, two hearts make one love. Two breasts for a single child. Two ovaries for a single uterus, two cheeks for a single face. And Two was God split into when he wanted to make Love

For ages I have been kept hungry and imprisoned in a cave. Now you are filling the parched deserted heart with heavenly ambrosia. Oh god, when divine energies flood in, what could mortal souls say. Now you are feeding this famished soul, whose intestine's capacity is just a hole of blue sky and a pinch of golden sun light. You are filling my whole with ocean of love when my heart's capacity is that of a newborn baby to suckle just a drop of its flavour.

I am every day morning brushing their teeth, oiling their hair, combing, powdering, milking them, feeding them, clothing them, caressing and fondling them, laugh with them, show them sky, birds, mongoose, owls, bats and all that my eyes could see, sing songs to them, kiss them with my loving heart. What not I do for them. Now when I open my heart and show to you, you say oh, it is only a shoe flower..."

WOMAN ON WOMAN'S DAY

how do you look today
are you sweet, did he say so?
are you soft, did he say so?
do you need others to say so?
woman of today sleep on your hand pillows
and sleep throughout night without any bellows

how is she today
the woman of international woman's day
is she pro man or anti men
is she virgin or un virgin
is she purdahed or pampered
wearing nothing but a bikini
does she cook or eats from hotel
does she count or ice creams lick

woman, who are you, are you mad
is she mad, stupid and idiotic
ashamed of this stupid day
i get up early morning and make tea
cook and bathe and run to office
come back at night, wash my vessels
sleep and again get up in the morning
and repeat my lovely duties of a woman
ha ha ha, do you follow me
i am a woman proud
so i cook cook cook
no book, book, book,
i tea make, tea make, tea make
snacks too if you please
and wash clothes, wash, wash,
all worries and tensions and guilts

i shall undertake
to a perfect T
am i an undertaker
but he says you, you, you
i am the cause of all miseries of all
i need treatment, electric or sticktric or handtrick
thank you vomiting womanhood, baby your man
and suckle him with love and drop the foetus
that is your job, you see you are a great woman of the day.

Editor's Note :- This poem was written by Lalitha Iyer (Hemangi Sharma) on March 7, 2016 – International Woman's Day. I had sent her a series of poems earlier that day. Her poems that day were partly in response to my poems.

I AM SINKING ON MY OWN DAY

I thought and thought and thought
of a way to celebrate this day
balloons oh no, we are big stuff
flowers, poor things, no not you
we are wonderful things, eh?
so i went into the kitchen and made some life
with my own song and my won dreams
with mongoose and crow and squirrels coming around
soon food was served, called my dog dachshund
come come come to me, let us celebrate together
where is he, he, he, he, i could not stop laughing
celebrations means men, men means wine
wine means woman, more women more wine
woman of the day, call your man
order wine, let us drink and sink.

Editor's Note :- This poem was written by Lalitha Iyer (Hemangi Sharma) on March 7, 2016 – International Woman's Day. I had sent her a series of poems earlier that day. Her poems that day were partly in response to my poems.

THE DEAD WIFE

A wife
is life;
smelling Coffees,
tasty Idlis,
sweets and
Jasmines
Bed of roses
pillows and cushions
evening melody
nights pleasure
hugging harmony
hanging symphony
loving unasked
kissing forever
tasty and pasty too..

when she dies
she takes her pies
kitchen is dessertsless
house is unkept
garden is unwatered
garbages stink
who Irons?

no more nights
nights are empty
filled with sleepless cigars
dawn alarms
come on, no more luxuries..

A PET'S LIFE

Poor thing
it watches through the caged doors
the smell of life
it pulls it from far afar
the scent of friends
souls of same fathers
peeps in
but pain grows more

Pet, are you, a pet?
inside the alien world
fattier and lonelier
with nobody to share
the natural desires of species
with none to mirror
what your heart rears.

in the house of a rich man
slave of whims and fancies
the pet pissed off for worldies
just alone, in the corner, the single heart
is it weeping or sad
or grieving for a counterpart
barking for familiarity
family and funds of simple hai's
a bite here, a push there, a pull up
and a push down
a pet is sad, pining alone
its urge to father groans
its mating heart moans.

BLEAK STREAKS

black and bleak
are the shadowed streaks
the light is on the other side
you are but the neglected maid

keenly drawing
the map of the figure
kissing at paths
where light is hindering

shadowy suspicious things
shadows causing ecliptic beings
reflecting the time of the day
dancing to the tune of the ray

shadow follows objects
as death follows living sects
what an unhappy ending
dismally following the golden ring

yet, a theory of Science
where light can't open the solids
and peep into the interiors
or is light is captivated
by beauty of inner airs.....?

MOTHER VALENTINE

I know love
but no lover
do I have
I love many
but they are so many
and I cannot choose
as I am all confused
Valentine card I have one
just to send for fun
I cant remember the one
who is my closest chum
When I asked my pal
said he love is like ink
it spreads in the surface linked
it cant touch a rod of solid
and taint it for long easily rid
on my teens my love
was in the air
kisses and dreams all afloat
as if i drift in a boat
with the waves and tides
taking me up to skies
and then dropping dead
I was no asked to bed
as I grew and got my son
love was in affection
in caring the baby
and tending his hobbies
as I grew, my body disappeared
and I became formless
my dresses did not to me donate
neither my dreams did mattered

I grew up, to love the poor
to suffer with the blind
and always be kind
to the bereaved
and that is being brave
oh my dear Valentine!
love has mellowed
now i see love in grey hairs too
arching spines and affected knees
love I found in toothless smiles
and twinkleless eyes
ugly urchins they ask me to kiss
they smell- the smell of love
the orphaned boys
with blank eyes and no toys
they call me ma
and I feel that ma
is love so beautiful
when you age and fill.

WHO LOVES MY MENSTRUATION BLOOD

I am bleeding
yes my heart
my holes
my eyes
and if i dont bleed
what sex will i be in lead?
if i dont bleed
my heart with no compassion
what human am I?
if i don't bleed
my eyes never red with grief
what soul am I?
I bleed
to create
my son
the universe
the motherhoods
they bleed to infants bring
it is in the blood
it is in the red
is it in the blood
is it in the red
or is it in the pain
creation-all soiled with blood
and blood the look of it
all reddy, vomiting from the womb
with no warning signs
just as it pleases
the ocean of blood
little by little to bring an infant
it clots into a cloth bag
to softly massage the spermovamed spot

inch by inch to snowball it
into limbs and head and heart
and lungs and eyes and nose
the names so called
oh the periods
the hell in the stomachs
the pain in the puberty
agony of a mother
sorrow of a shelterless woman
tragedy of divine births
we bleed to create
we create in blood
mammals we mammals
we white blooded suckle
and red blooded pickle
in pain, in blood all life
all births constrained to knife.

MOTHER'S GIFT

little by little
I grew up
and smelt the sweetness of life
in my mother's cuddles
waking up in the morning
she used to fondle my face
and kiss my lips holding in her embrace
as I woke up from my dreams
my lazy lousy head drowsing
she will coo into my ears
that birds are calling my names
she will make me feel
as if the earth has dawned
just for me and just for her
stroking my cheeks
every new bird and new bloom
she will point out for me
and make my thoughts lively
her dosas, her idlis and her chutneys
every food tasted from her inner love
she oozed with an angelic grace
the coffee she poured, the bajjis she fried
the kolams she made and baths she does
everywhere she went, she spilled some aroma
i licked the world around, its loveliness
as mum used to plate it in my bosom
she died, she died leaving me the legacy
of how she viewed the world around
how the sparrow chirps
with tiny feet and tiny mouth
how it fed its chicks
and how it found its home

and made the place a Rome
how the clouds carried away
secrets of fertility
till the curved peaks
they crushed against and rained
how the full moon on love
with the suckling earth that lustily fed
upon her silky breasts raving mad
the raging maid the ocean tide
how the longing waves wanted to hug
the earth and all her siblings
jealous of earth loving not her
but the beings on her womb
how she mustered strength to march
and kill one by one the poor things
oh, there is more things silly to say
my world around and within
too silly yet they are mother's gift
mother till her last breath
still in her rest do speak
to me of volumes when I delight
seeing the simple wonders spinning light.

I SMELL MY MOTHER

I am old now;
my limbs stiff
my heart stuck
emotions ruined
memories wiped
youth deleted
passions filtered
reactions checked
attractions killed
actions frozen
words refined
cautioned behaviour
commercial sentences
competitive lies
fatigued brain
and fashionless spine

As I weep alone
sobbing for a soul mate
I could watch the mangoose mum
with her little love
tailing to her tail
what a glued affection it is!
It is a beauty
to feast upon
the sight of oozing love
love sans conditions and intentions
entwined mom and baby mangoose
stop, stopped, sit, sat
hush, silent, alert, into the hole.
what a beauty
the love coverage

in the material world of promotions
no cash can encash mothers love

Watching through my windows to greens
I lick the treat of mother's love
shielding harm of alien predators
always you can spot a mother from others
her life is a red signal, lit throughout
no, means no, the world is insecure
the message deeply injected
generations to generations
mother's message is crystal clear;
dont trust strangers
watch out unusual sounds
and shelter my babe shelter
protect, my darling, protect
dancing with her darlings
she will, when green covers her full and filling
I smell my mom in mangoose mom
Oh dear, mom is God on earth
fathers mother mothers
yet, mothers are mothers dear.

SHAME OF WOMB

Who will bear the shame of Carrying?
He who bore the Cross
or he who adore the Crescent
or he who herded the sheep
or he who roads the weep.

Who will bear the shame of a Womb?
The husband who seeded her
the child who is embedded in her?
the nature which breeded her?
or the culture which feeded her?

They lashed her for being a Widow
they bled her for sharing without vow
they whipped her for crossing the line
she sipped only the cup of her Creator's wine.

She was beaten up in public
a mute, silent, cowardish republic
she was ripped open, a budding mother
her womb shall curse the kingdom and others

the pain she bore, oh God forbid no more
shall any woman suffer, in her passions tower
unknowing the cause and cure, they tore her apart
the temple of birth, the Mosque of Life and Church under cover

those who know not their mother
or mother's pain and stained shiver
beat her for bearing a child with no father
what is in a father, but a knot donkeyed to devour...

they did a job that motherless men do
they killed the fatherless babe which they have save to do
they violated the Creator's Code
for no reason they transgressed the basic moral mode

to bear the fruits a tree has liberty
birds of feather weather the pollens every tree
plants breed, animals freed, birds create, dogs deviate
nature seeds, nature has weeds,
the killer weeds grew more wrongly
the creator's deeds cursed as weeds.

the man who seeded did not stop
the men who witnessed did no job
the men who beat her heartless brutes
and the God who Spermed the life forms silent
did not afford her ease and escape route
was he ashamed to own his name,
who bleeded her to sprout from age's the same

MEMORIES OF MY MARRIAGE

We married
when I was a Queen
in my Teens
and he the Lord
of my Passions.

As days rolled on
and my our ways split
the pillows of lust
burst open by rage of fist
and thus we parted
the knot was untied

Again I marry
no more a Queen
with heart not heavy
mind not breezy
steps clear
and thoughts easier

Married did I
with dreams rosy
Divorced am I
well versed
with the laws of Nature

Now, to company
to smile and chatter
seek I rather
a friend with no hopes
but only a trust in shape.

At Old age
a man is no more knight
and woman a Queenly sight
everything could be combined
life still meant love and sunshine.

GIRL BY THE STREET

Insensitive,
Cruel.

Women passed by,
saw a woman struggling
on the street to give birth.

They did nothing..
They did nothing.
They did nothing.
Women ???

She is poor.
She is ugly.
She has no home.
She has no food
or water.

umbilical cord not cut
the child cries on the street.
and the people pass by
even women pass by
cruel is this nation
insensitive, the people.
brutal, carless,
loveless.

Umbilical cord is still attached,
crying as it lies wrapped
in its mother's dress.

Are we human beings
or devil's children?
Do we have mercy in us?
Do we have love in us?

God, your poor die on the streets.
God, your poor give birth on the streets.
God where are you?
Humans where are you?

Poet's Note :- A 17-year-old girl who was abandoned by her family after falling pregnant gave birth on a street in India, according to local media reports. The girl gave birth on the side of the road in Chandil, a town in the state of Jharkhand in eastern India. She was said to have been less than 100 meters from a health center. A video published purportedly shows the girl hunkered down with her baby in the street as cars and motorcycles pass by. The newborn, whose umbilical cord is still attached, is pictured crying as it lies wrapped in its mother's dress.

PART – V

OLD AGE CURSE

THE FLICKERING LAMP

BE A CO-TRAVELER

Caught between the devil and the deep sea I am dying. Either I suffer from bereavement or drowned and soaked I get wet forever eternally drowned. What to do, I am too much in love that I am burning with love. O Lord, guide me to the other shore...

A poet is the one who keeps plenty of secrets and sometimes spontaneously he begins to sing in his soul and then writes them down. When he forgets himself and writes it becomes a poem which touches and sometimes converts the reader.

Do not first buy, but just be a co-traveler, in the roads of life, in the road to heaven, have a passer-by who shall forever be a companion who needs no explanation for smiling or crying. Have a hand, that knows when to support, have a heart that knows when to throb, have a lip that knows when to kiss or not to. Have a hug that knows when to or not to. Do not buy, but be a fellow good Samaritan. After all life is only a ladder to reach God's paradise.....

SUNSET OF MY LIFE

Farewell to all living things
to all those which respond
Sunset has come
Darkness, pure dark
night has overcome
all our miseries and sadness
with the lovely world of sleeps
as the sun sets
my melancholy steps up
i feel i am alone
sandy shores become alien
as if they have swiftly changed
transformed into some giant dragons
rearing to gulp me and mine
all golden dreams gone with sunset
dying songs, dying music, dying lights
sunset is so tragic, yet people ache to see
setting sun in reddish aura
passing ships and plying boats
many a fast day ends into nothing
but sunset, only sunsets could close the days
every life, sweet and sour, beautiful and ugly
angels, terrorists all will die one day
at the altar of destiny
all suffer truths equally
when the egoes strut and stand
and voices echo with kindly bands
I feel the silence that quietly says
no, no, this will not do
time will tell you what i mean
tide will kill the men of greed
all the loved ones taken one by one

all great men died asleep
some were burnt in stakes
some in gas chambers
but Hitlers never cry
and Jews always sob
remembering forever the bereaved brethren
the man who lost is always lost
his grief is forever his only grief
for one who has heart always feel
either for him or his countrymen
Sunsets speak of rising suns
yet dawn is far off
night is cold and killing
every freezing second of night is ticking
slowly, very slowly
as if it will never end.

NEW POETRY FOR MY OLD AGE

No meaning could I find
for living
yet I wake up in the morn
cook and comb like a doll
bathe and bake on a call
the only thing I feel good
is to sleep and let loose ground
Can u explain y I live
my hairs turn grey now
my limbs all tardy
pain is pinching my buttocks
my bones are steel rods
jutting from the drying flesh
I still am alive
could you tell me why I am
who am I?
my parents are dead
my roots already cut
my child does not understand
what my confusion is all about
I am asking questions
but cannot find a single one answer
money is not my need
my need is the reason for this deed
I did not find god
my searches were scant for reward
yet after digging a lot of mud
from my mind I feel I am no more
the person I thought me like sky
slipped through my fingers
hours are not filled with romance
days don't take me to songs of strings

I just don't feel that I belong to any of the things
that is here, that cheers and bears
my house is not mine
and my body too repels me at times
i wonder y I carry this trunk
which adds pain to my junk
be positive, yes, be positive
yet what poetry when clothed in finest silk
could alleviate poverty of mind and matter
money can buy things external
what will buy you living urge within
my dears, still i like a kid of five and one
keep on staring at the crowd effects
and grow numb and frozen with every day.

Note :- single letters "u" and "y" for you and why are typical of Lalitha's
(Hemangi Sharma) poetry.

AGELESS PAIN IN ACHING LIMBS

the grey locks
unlocked them
from the look of frocks
to the look of rocks
the talk of a child
to the babble of childish ride

the same moon
it is stirring not my soul
the same sea
it screens away
romantic maids
in to oblivion

the dying mind
the dead life
perverted thoughts
pessimistic acts

aching limbs
ageless pains
forlorn hearts
jerky self
in rhapsody

what is more
that todays are yesterdays
and tomorrows are yesterdays
and yesterdays are timeless space
they appear and reappear
born and reborn

every body reincarnated
every love replayed
every child respermed
every act reacted
every heart repumped
in full vitality

from the dead soil
which is not really dead
from my mother's wishes
born are my son's tresses...

LOSS OF MY SELF

Slowly
I am ageing
start was slow
but pace is fast

I did not realise
only when the hair greyed
did I wonder
that I am matured

It is a tragedy
to ripen is to fruit
to mature is fatal
though maturity is wisdom

Slowly I have lost interest
yes, my urge to dress up
and enjoy life afresh
is losing momentum
and I am lagging
unwanted

It all began
with gradual loss
of identification
of beings of either gender
I started treating
Hes as Shes
and Shes as Hes
as if what use
the difference could make?

It is a retreat
all battles have been won
no more passions
lurking underneath
stirring unwanted emotions.

My limbs are crazy
they behave painfully drowsy
the lust for life
it is in the snail pace strife
I miss nothing,
but suddenly everything is gone
blank is my page
ink in letters have evaporated
the perfume in the bottle
it has become perfect air
no softness in the texture
no satin in the hair touch
no more my skin
reacts to delicate moisturisers
I just feel
I am a clueless camphor
distilled in the air,
bodyless, odourless
past melted into......

nowhere.

MELTING INTO NOTHINGNESS

I am melting
into nothing
as I realise
truths disguised

My name
was sweet
when I learnt it first
as I grew up fast

now as I age
I have paged
thousands of names
meaning nothing only games

my name is lost
in memory's chart
I wonder but for post
what my address hosts.

My figure is fading
my limbs are paining
my control is lost
I am disintegrating

My parts are replaced
my lens, knees all laced
when every organ is transplanted
who am I, with my body implanted

My poetry is somebody'
my feelings I share with many

my ideas are imported from books
my emotions are only silly stuff.

I walk the traces you left
I think again what you spoke
I cook the recipe of yours
I dream nothing but what you saw.

I am melting down to nothing
nothing new is born
nothing is mine I a Popcorn
moment's foam, bubble of seconds.

PAIN OF AGE

It pains
to age
not in body
but in mind

when the lovely dawn
no more cheers me
when my fragile limbs
ache more at morn

when the splashing wetness
make me fear of fevers
when the dashing kids
kill me with painful cramps

when my mind is done
I am done
no more brains
but only chains

when the world sings
I am afraid of noise
when the world dances
I am hating actions

When the food I eat
poisons me
when hope ends up
into nothing

but only nothing.

I AM SINKING WITHIN

Nobody notices
nobody discovers
but I am sinking
yes sinking

kinetic movements
are all fine
but potential energies
have started sapping
out of time

nobody could feel it
but only me myself
just this dawn
i realise now
i am done..

the store bed of life
has started receding
i am shivering
for drugging urge

nobody finds it out
not even your man
every day your duties go
but i know, i am swiftly slow

inner oxygen levels are on decline
mind is meditating into nothing
i am sinking, no more excuses
i am waning, no more pretensions

what is there, after all
life is just a manuscript
corroded by time
eroded by passions

my page is but an illusion
since any page may be mine
what is written is out of fashion
interpretation is anybody's choice

every page is mine
when emotions tear
when truths trumpet
i am a carpet finished.

A LEPER'S LUST

I wish to embrace you
but I am a leper
my diseases will spread
into your bed
I want to see you naked
not just without clothes
I want to peep into you
and penetrate your inner recess
and find out the smelling soul
sleeping within
all innocent and calm
your bed I cant tread
my wounds are bleeding badly
your lips I wont touch
mine are bitten by poisonous teeth
the air I cant pollute
my germs are deadly and irritate
you are to me
a mind of hopes and dreams
I am but only
a corpse of dying sickness
In you I see the beauty of life and Origin
I am but only a wretched Kind
my limbs are giving
my sight is dwindling
I harp on humanity
just a hope in divinity
together we will be the greatest blunder
no peacock mates with pigs eating wastes
your plumes are lovely
I am only wallowing ugly
your lines are sweet

my mind is on retreat
your world is beautiful
mine dirty and horribly real
you are in a bed of Roses
my thorny bush no sleep to me risks
I am parched and pennied
you are the King of Oceans
and counting stars in your purses
Night is Yours
and moonlight you robe
Day is Mine
my labour's sweat is my rhyme
dropp by dropp it drenches my time
and the pinching Summer pricks my signs
your love will melt
when you see my sight
ugly face
ugly eyed
ugly dress
ugly life
in rotten food
I thrive for livelihood
you have pictures
of Angels in your mind
but, I am a crooked oldie thing
my face is full of patches
and body complete with arches
I speak words impolite
and curse at every mortal
for my life is beset with Ordeals
I am black in colour
and my breast are burnt with scars
my legs are strutting from hips
two sticks of knitting needles

they ache and pain and the disc of spine
it kills me when I rest

I have no splendour
nor in life I wonder
I am the woman of seeds
sell my body unheeded
to me love counts not
love is only a romantic notion
it's the recluse of
silly woman of Riches
they proud and pretty
walk with silks flimsy
dress to reveal more
and reveal in dresses sore
myself am a Woman in beds
my dreams are infested with blood
and sickening Odours of men of mud
my days I painfully suck
to spend I have nothing
I am just a spent stuff.

Note :- Initial capitalisation of words like Ocean, Odour, Origin, Riches and Kind etc I do not fully understand. Lalitha (Hemangi) never revealed to me the meaning. I leave them to readers to guess. Summer and Day refer to the person she truly loved.

A GRAIN OF SAND

I am but reduced
to a grain of sand
lying in Ocean land
I was up at the mountain
peaking at the peaks
speaking to the skies
the crowning glory
sparkling snow capped

at the height of vanity
I danced to the valleys
proud of my beauty
a mountain I was
now a sand grain
from stone to pebble
reduced on my rumble

now only a sand
but years have added
in me wisdom with kind
I understand
that my life is a mission
to discover
the link between
skies and sand....

BUT PROMISES ARE LATE

Life days are over
Sun is about to set;
body is paining
the blazing rays are golden
it is dusk
limbs are faltering with fatigue;
smell of farewell lingers
age reasons the arrival of death.

When life reaches fifty
the seesaw is midway
reasoning snaps
cords of romance
seasoned memory
reminds foolish fantasies are stupid
yet the blue sea is tempting
distant ships are sailing
night is charming
stars are twinkling
moon is sweet and melodies lute
dusk is full of promises late.

WAS I BORN FOR THIS DAY

In this troubled world
I am born untold
years have past
my story is lost
like a pebble
in a rivulet
my originals are nomore
my mum is in heaven
or shining amidst stars
my dad is on his way too
the body is shaking a bit
i am nearing my forty and slit
the message is not found
in my books of school
nor bags of Office
neither the path I walk
nor the men I shake hands with
they all laugh and smile
with fake faces they sleep
fake faces they wake up
their words are only echoes
their talks speak of nothing
I am waiting for the message
on the wall of life
i am standing here
strutting out like an ugly pillar
to be rubbed off
like a scar oozing with puss
i have to be healed
or i will worsen
will you send me the message
y was i born

the music just heals
yet, its voice is not in feels
I am asking, y am I
down the river
it has a meaning
the bee
it collects honey
the wind
it brings rain clouds
the sun
it is known to all
it is the universal source
of energy and life
but y I
Y i a foreigner to this land
here I see people in-sanity's end
i was innocent
and smiled sweet to the wind
they took my innocence
and made me incoherent
crowned with no glory
i feel all this misery
dear friends of poems
could u read the wall message
could u spell it and massage
me heart full of woes and age
y, y, y you and i were born.

Note :- Single letters "u", "i", "y" standing for You, I and Why are typical of
Hemangi Sharma's literary style.

LIFE IS DRAINING

my life
it throbs
cut off from divine
It exists
till the urge persists

the energy is draining
I am sinking
Soon the day of melting
arrives in horses stumping

I am vanishing
my thoughts dissembling
slowly i cant realise
the crowd and its ways

passions erased by maturing years
sadness of impending insecurities bear
my identity I am loosing
I wake up and sleep chasing
dreams without stuff and spacing...

THEN I WANT TO DIE

Then I want to die
when your love never dies
when my dreamy nights
fly past, swifter than light

Then I want to die
when my senses swim
in the hands of invisible Rum
I reduced to a black hole's whim.

Then I wanted to die
when you cradle me
back to innocence
bathe me with mum's essence...........

BEFORE I DIE

Before I die
I want to meet you
like a kid
aching to touch
the toys in rows
along the market windows

Before I die
I want to touch you
with the soft hands
of a touch me not plant
a last touch that shall end me up
a last attempt to die in somebody's cup.

Before I die
I want to tell you
that you are my dawns
and dusks and dreams
I was with you all these years
and I grew up with those hours
when I was inhaling your pours

Before I die
I wish I could hold
that moment when I could see
in your looks the golden glee
that make my existence sure
and life immortal and pure
to ashes into the real pyre
into the flames of consuming tear....

LET ME NOW DIE

I dont know what to do
I am reduced to nothing
my aims are no more sound
my goals dont bound
I am just wondering
my body within shivering

my senses devalued
my passions crystallized
my sentiments criticized
my ideas centrifugalized

good and bad
sabotaged
all goods are cowardish
all bads are gold medalists

where is God?
playing hide and seek
or seeking me
with as much vigour
as I seek him

may be in Crores
of Galaxies
he is staying
in one
and seeking from the other end
and I from this end

all physical nudities
echoing stupidity

and mocking at me
The entire Galaxies
are budding in my inner self
I am shivering
I am quivering
I am trembling
I am lost, dont know
what to do
all tangibilities
killing me from within
about to burst
about to worst
I am like the Species girl
transforming into something
I dont know, choiceless
I am not dying, no
I am metamorphosised
Oh, the pain of changing
from within, the cosmic attacks
Oh...............I am pained
but words are meaningless
words are wastes
they dont express
what I am undergoing
the spell is cast
Let me die unconscious........

BEFORE MY LAST SLUMBER

Charms of youth are wiped
when darkness sets in

The rosy hues are lost
in the depths of evening sky
when the eyes loses sight
and ears never melodies delight

When fatigue strikes the limbs
when faces twitch in painful lumps
youth is gone and old age groans
yet who has wiped those smiles of lawn........

Every morn I wonder
if it is the last day to wake up
Every night I wonder
if it is my last slumber not to open
the looking eyes to see the best
in earth and above and beneath

It is sickening
to loose hours
when hours are so sweet
It is horrifying
to add seconds
when seconds are depressing

Oh god!
give me love
to love the innocent doves
give me smiles
to smell the morning dews.............

MY MOMENT OF GRIEF

The parting moment
hands want to squeeze
the warmth to share
like a gentle breeze
the lips want to kiss
marking the moment of miss
like a whispering leaf
in the wilderness in grief
to express its lonely hours
to come and to come and to come
saving the present
and shaving off the brutal future
securing the right to excuse
other interruptions
the Saga of tales
storied into the looks
confirming, consoling, comforting
catching up with, contorting into forms
dipping into emotions endless
when they parted
we saw the pain
and disdain
written in her cheeks
stained in hug stain
as she waved
her fragile breasts caved
into her sobbing chest
her aching wish
writhed to push her flesh
into motions contrary
to what normal leg could carry....

could you, would you, should you
all questions stilled
in the fixed stare
gazing with disbelief
the separating second stunns
mobility of life
and ability to reason
stopping with the sinking looks
storming with an urging beg
desperate lips part in disbelief
silenced letters choking in grief........

HOUR OF DEATH

the hours are counted
my days are numbered
this may be my last step
this may be my last talk

wonder whether I will wake up
and see the morning buttercups
enjoy the hot tea and breakfast
pack up to Office like the rest

thinking of the illness lurking
behind the skin of every being
I wonder how long will I last
thought my limbs are very fast

somebody told me in some book I got
that live as if you are living the last but second thought
and that makes you fast and passionate
attached to your duties and appointments with haste

this is the penultimate moment
next inhaling breath shan't come out
the beating heart will stop and shut up
the pulsating arteries shall deny the aching drop

see the ants their life is brief
any second your stand and finish
the poor ends up none to grieve
see the bees and butterflies
that gathers nectar and flutters with wings
in the golden sunshine they give you things
that is so natural and simply baffling

yet, they live but a few hours to days

the undying being is only Love
it lives in those hearts that crave
to feel the tender emotions
with touching tears and passion
god is love, they said
we hung it in the display board
but indeed is he in the love form
lovely too and loving too
he is eternal since he is loving
till the day you love somebody
he does not dies and lives in some body
the demon king thence ordered the priests
not to chant the god's name lest he lives
in the thoughts of men and hearts of thoughts
the heart of love is made of molten love
it is adhesive and eternally embedded
in the pages of the Creation unwedded.

LURE OF DEATH

It pulls me
egging me to go ahead
the wild is so fantastic
I cant resist, but yield.
The song of the greens
the whistling unknown birds
the piercing Cuckoo
pinching my heart's youth
I cant resist, but yield
I have to go ahead and see.
When the lightning cuts across the heavenly breast
you feel the spark embering upon your chest
when the thunder roars across the satanic clouds
you shiver with the mysterious fear feeling the deads
Rain, felling the earth with ferocious tide
Painless strains plunges me into stinging abides.
Wild, exciting, enflaming the inner being
the esctastic birds, emperors of free love
rippling ponds and walls of wave-urging ocean beds
like the giant mouth of the monster of fairy tales
ponds like the golden curls of mermaid unfurled
in their green palms strewn across I stuck upon
wonder how many gossips are hidden on leave faces
and nature creeps into my being with her trump card
Death is very attractive and tempting
it lures every time you face it with new inventions
every death full of new blind convictions
groping in the dark with the body of emotions
tears cascading down and weeping loneliness penetrating
impregnant with the stunning seed of truth stupifying
with every new death, new life is born within
and the every death crushes me with an upper hand

and captivates me with its charming pride
once again totally helpless
abandoned with emptiness
I start drawing a new map
to measure her ambiguities
amazingly clear
she wipes off all old traces
and new faces of death dances
upon the wild once more

The charm of life is death
and death frightens you
just so beautifully.

WAKE ME NOT

Dont wake me up
trouble me not
with your songs
bang not my door
with your knocks
I am too weak
to wake up
I should die

Dont touch me
my limbs are weak
my passions fragile
down deep within
my pulses cold
my senses old
Dont feel me
I am senseless bane.

Dont tease me
with your smiles
my wrinkled life is full of fails
I should die or I shall cry
I am baking within
scorched by pinching suns
I should die or my sluggy
feelings creep to stinks.

MY ASHES IN GANGES

The ashes were heaped
and the pot was carried
to mix it with the Ganges
and make the dead one holy

soon an image jumped out
from the flowing stream of river
it had a face of haggard stretch
yet bore some features of me wretch

I stooped to see the things clear
yes, it was my aged figure
my bones and ribs crushed to pieces
i could see my body done to powder

i could see the grave and the pyre burning
my living body was put to fire
i could see all tomorrows
they galloping todays mingle with

the shaky legs and shivering hands
oh, its me, its me
the screwing eyes and stooping back
oh, its me, its me

i am the body in the pyre
i am the ashes into the river
Ashes to Ashes my matter disperses
My spirit is watching the traveler's desirous.........

PART – VI

PRISONER OF MY CELL

SPIDER IN OWN WEB

You are the god I was searching for. What more could I say. If a human heart could be divine, if god is born as human and if you could sense his heart, then it is yours. I had never in the horizon of my dreams horizon ever dreamed that a man could be as divine as you. And to be truthful, the man behind the curtain of god, I kneel before him too.

Never, never shall I betray you. Though a lamb you are a lamp. You are my dearest Jesus. You are the lone light at the top of my temple. And I shall never never even show you any cross at all. You see, I am the biggest cross in the world. Then you know, this cross if you wear, if you endure, then no cross will be more difficult for you to bear.

The cross will be thrown out soon. And it will have to walk to the cross bearer in the middle of night. Hope the cross bearer will come riding a white peacock to me....

You are my be-all and end-all.

PRISONER OF MY CELL

up and down
i can go
right and left
let me march
ha ha ha
friends come and go
like winds of rain
they gush in jolly
yes, life is busy
canteens are funny
like dreamland honey
they are draped with coffee
dripping with teas and teens free
yet, unhappy prisoner am i
my wings clipped free
they did not ask me to pay the price
but wings did they take
furry coat they made
to clothe their happy pets
i am not alone i did say
lots and lots of jelly fishes
all swimming big breasted
a sight any killer whale loves
to swim around and dive to gulp
poor jelly fishes.

but mine is a different thing
i am a dying fish
with not fin or feelers or gills
little oxygen is enough
but that little is biasedly pent up by kingpins
pirates have landed upon my ship

and captain has sunk us to black sea magic
in the middle of the red sea he told me
i will wait and you pair with me there
i am dying in black seas, how to go to red sea
jailed inside the witched cabins
with a hawker and a hobbly-nobbly joker
hawker shall pawn even my heart
joker shall joke even about my ooops
i chatter, chatter, chatter all my day
to escape the dreadful clutter of the day
to ride the sun and end the day
i in clutter bake my bread, all sweet and jammed
creamed and scrambled eggs taste better
but the butcher never shaves his beard
and his prison looks are made of empty utters
he found the thief, he found the thief
may be tomorrow he shall free
all the empty prisoners alive.

Editor's Note :- Hemangi Sharma wrote it on March 10, 2016 when she
first began corresponding with me under fake ID of Lalitha.

SIGH OF A FALLEN LEAF

do you think a fallen leaf is sad?
the passerby sigh
oh the fallen leaf has no life.
the mother tree shrugs
no more hugs, not mine you are.
the poor fallen leaf dusted self
and looked upon the specks of mud
that gathered upon her breast
once upon a time, she felt
she was at the top of the tree
and haughtily she looked down
at the earthy things, clay and dust
oh, they are too ugly to be gowned
she shrunk from their sight
and unfriended their thoughts too
now, as she lay upon the dust bed
she felt the warmth of dust specks
how could they love her she wondered
after all she had shunned them when she shone
upon the tree top in the glowing sunlight
and breezing sweet wind
now, as she lay destined to die
her fair weather friends all deserted
her beauty and love, all titanicked
she looked upon the specks of dust
with such wisdom and heart of blood
oh to be touched by the hands of dust
to be kissed by the earth so loving
life is real grounded to rest
she licked them with true spirit
reality, oh reality, weeping hard
thou are wide open at nature's silent yard.

VOICE OF NOTHINGS

It was the night of nothings
silence caved in with everything

feelings smothered by numbness
sayings ruined by repetitions

she lied in the bed of death
with passions and compassions all wreathed

her voice could no more be heard
no sound could be uttered by the lips upturned

what was youth, only a memory
what was life, only a summary of zeroes

green and dry, everything sailed by
now, no tears, no fears, no cheers

when the spellings of destiny
twisted by dictionaries

the voice chilled by death
could no longer warm the hearth....

NIGHT BEFORE DAWN

it was very bleak
the night before
the air was cold
and damp
no leaf stirred
no life aired
any living urge

thoughts scattered
emotions battered
the bride awaited
for dawn to break

passions weighed
profusions stayed
dreams were escaping
energy sweeping

no song to cheer up
no bird to sound up
no hand to hold on
no band too cold it was

the bride sat upon
the barren rock of life
with breast full of oceans
full of tidal confusions

it was the night of darkness
night before final surrender
either life will be wedded
or the body shredded

it was stillness
killing the raging blindness
blind was the future
blind was present
past was blinking
like a blinding mission

sinking moods
stifling words
heart listens
to every throb
upon the surface
of earth, air and water

dawn was far off
the bride was dying
her hopes were waning
it was a wish tied to the heart
secretly prized unseen to eyes
freezing reality started dewing
and she started shivering
when truths started barking

midnight hours
jamming chords of power
every second was sinking
into the hopeless linking

transparent thoughts trailed
vanishing images hailed
the flicker died out
and silence worded out
thus ends the night before dawn....

SONGS OF MY PAIN

My soul is the home
of a wounded butterfly

It sings in prayer
at dawn and dusk

It sings its sorrows
on autumn's leaves

Heal not my wounds!

Let my songs be born
from the pain of my wounds.

MY CUP OF TEARS

I sat to collect my tears
in an earthen cup
and hid it carefully
behind my smiling mask

I hid my sufferings
and grinned like a bird
at everyone on the way

They thought i was happy
but it was a simple lie

I hid behind my mask
my painful bleeding heart
everything is torn inside me
they saw only the mask

The memory of those who
cheated me purposely
carved my soul and heart
I cried silently and prayed

My prayer to christ was
Thank you Lord for helping
me to join in your passion.

They crucified me and i bleed.

Today i wanted to pray
God forgive them
but I am a simple human being.
Please give me your forgiving mind.

CAGED BIRD SINGS

The caged bird sings
songs of her sorrows

They are sad songs
they reflect a life
of stunted dreams
of joy and freedom
which it has lost

The caged bird sings
from depth of pain
in her aching heart.

RIVER OF MY GRIEF

I am sitting
on the banks of river
the river of life
that flows through trials
the pebble of thoughts
i put and wait
to hear the ripples
and peep of fishes
in hope of food
the school seeks my slips
I sit here in cool breeze
yet, somebody
far away I can feel
I can trust
myself touching
some hands or heart
of distant body
a body of love
of life and drive
It fills me with armies
of silk coated lies
he sends across borders
swords of stylish steel
sharp and killing with feel
somewhere the pebbles
I drop are too drowning
and ripples are sometimes
too fast and untimely
they splash the water
across my face
and my body drenched
with my thoughts in streams.

DARK ALLEYS OF MY NIGHT

It is dark
I am blinded
my alleys are lightless
fear is creeping
a child's fear it is
to hug to somebody
strong and forceful
who could take me up
to the heights of heavens
and tell me that life is all even
i started crying
my prayers were over
i did not stars see
neither the moon
it was under the clouds
somebody is hiding
behind the walls
I know
I know it is to kill me
or rape me brute
I started weeping
afraid of shouting
for my sound echoed
down the alleys
and I started shaking
shivering with aching
that was me
a Child of five
slowly I grew
my tears dried
fears no more fried
my tenders sleepless

now I know
that the night
is as romantic
and beautiful
as the full-lit day
that it is not the end
it is the way to the dawn
that sleep is sexy
and dreams are blessings
that cot is foamy
and pillows are lovely
they soothen the brains
and stifle the pains
I know now
my world is not dark
the light of Sun
is not the end of the run
my hopes are sealed
s they are concealed
in the deepest spots
where life stream gurgles
and God's cream suckles....

MY TEARS ARE DIAMONDS

I collected my tears.
They were diamonds.

The whole night i cried.
Early morning I went
to the holy temple
to offer my tears
as my great offerings.

I have nothing else to offer.
My tears are my pure gifts.

I SAW FEAR IN HER EYES

dark storm was gathering
in her soul's recesses
breaking into thick
loud thunders

I saw fear in her eyes
as the sky fell
she screamed aloud

There was no one
in the wilderness
to hear her scream

but me

in her eyes
I saw myself
Screaming aloud.

PRAYER AND SATAN

I counted the rosary
praying by the window
on my knees

dawn to twilight
I prayed alone
lost in the count
of rosary beads

The more i prayed
on those holy beads
the more i was tempted
by the very devil.

I AM UGLY, I AM DIRTY

My Lord,
I am ugly,
yes dark and ugly
yet, my heart is sweet
I am dirty
yeah bruised and dirty
yet, my thoughts are neat

I live in a street
but I don't retreat
my bed is in shreds
but I dont suffer asleep
with strangers who need
one for this night
one for the next

I live in scatters
yet natural my air is
the man I shall bed with
his arms my garland be
let him be a beggar
yet, our dreams shall castles
build in the atmosphere
which rains for us too
and pains though I undergo
but parent not kid
whose father's name he knows not

As an honest maid
in genuine love
I invite you to my streets
and activate your muscles

and work like a man
just a man you should be
honestly sweat
for all you eat
and marry in modesty
and then come to my bed
which is in the shreds
among the garbage feds..

SELF MADE PRISONS

a child thinks
God is above the clouds
he sleeps and crowds
to bless the earth
he sends the rain
to cheer the hearts
he sticks up the stars
to soothen the sleepless
he sends the moon
to silver the yards
with her lengthy cord

a maid thinks
the man with the moustache
and deep looks haunting
could put her upon top of the tree
that touches the heavens
that he could win her
the world she aspired forever
that his words are coins
and touches are wands
springing ecstastic bangles
from the hips of her jungles

Gods get carried away
by winds of strong forces
women get married away
to realise life's true farces
illusioned with a single being
we cheat ourselves of the silvery lining
our imaginations artistically slave us
and we defeated by self-made prisons.......

PART – VII

I SEEK FREEDOM

LIGHT AT END OF TUNNEL

HOUSE OF MY BELOVED

Whatever you give, you receive in thousand folds. If you give with a pure heart and a pure mind with pure intentions, when you are sharing your love, your whole being will be flooded with that Love.

Now I know, when I met you, that there is this god whom I had prayed all these days. See, with meeting you the whole thing is over. Now living is the plum of cake. You are asking will I eat the cake or not. See, if I eat it will be finished. So I will only lick and keep on licking so that the cake is okay. I can have the cake and lick the cake.

I want to go to my Beloved's house and die there itself, never to come back again. But when you go to the moon, you will realise that moon is like earth only.....

Love is not mine, neither yours, you cannot possess it, nor can you dispossess it. Every pure mind is permeable to love that flows through it. Like water that runs across when there are no dams, like rivers that flow through forests and wilds, love just flows through hearts when there is no barrier.

I SAW YOU ON MY SILENT STREET

I missed me
when I missed you
you who live in my heart
and beat in my pulse
and sink into my stream
and bloodly mingle with my dreams.

I saw you only yesternight
when a strange dream woke me
up and alight
I saw u in the silent streets
roaming for some resting needs

you were the silent beggar
half crazy, and me too
you begged for things seen
and I beg for emotions unseen
your things are in the shop
my alms in heavenly harps

I missed the looks
your sight of life
kissed in tight
they speak of ages plight
of hunger, halt and nameless horror
they sink into me and stir fires to core

my heart is weighing
I missed my life
I lost to carry with
the hope and honey spread
with trust in living ahead

I am terribly sad
something is killing me mad
i need the solace of a language
that shall enter my person caged
and free to lands amazed

I had missed me
when I had missed you
on my silent street
I was the lone traveler
you who lived in my heart
became a co-traveler.

IN SEARCH OF TRUTHS

All of us wander
in search of same truth
some in wine
some in dine
music is my relief
dancing is your life
she lives in swims
he lives in books
yet all of us we are
in search of same truths
we do pray
though astray
we pray in tongues
new and alien
in myriad altars
of shapes anew
we do kneel
sob and shriek
in fear and hope
in shame and anguish
yet, we all mutter
in languages different
that we may be salvaged
from this world
full of changing colours
where truth is deep
yet, to find is a life sweep
we all walk
side by side
destinations final
we ache for one goal

in search of same truths
we did wander together
yet the terrorist
and the wounded
all took different weapons
and prayed for a holy land
when we all in the caravan
the learned and the pupil
the master and the student
all at different stages
at different levels of truth
different wisdom zones
tuned our minds and hearts
to different cosmic velocities
we almost half knew
that we were all
on the same path.

VOICES OF SILENCE

Sweet thoughts
through my window
floated in slowly
putting me to sleep

my heart was sad
my days were bad
moments gloomy
mind very lonely

I prayed
on my bed
for some messages
no e mails
no alerts no sms
just from heavens
some soothing lines

As in faith
I touched the point of feel
when my tears rolled down
and sobs tided
into uncontrollable shakes
the lovely voice
like a silk fabric
covered my heal

with a touch of mother
I slowly wiped
my inner being
for a moment
my grief was gone

and I listened
kneeling unbelieving
the magic of heavens

I slowly undressed
before my mirror
looking inward
and magic entered
my body's pores

it filled the air
with messages
from my past
urging me to go

ahead...
ahead....

MY LAST WISH

I wish
my dear ones
never go into earth's
mounted heaps

that their lovely soft bodies
don't stink with stench
of wormed dead ones

that the dreams
in those eyes I behold
don't vanish suddenly
into burning pyres
to become ashes
and cold ashes

I wish my mum lives
in some sweet heavens
with some starry angels
dancing to her delight

I wish my boy
be a sunny boy always
never grows into an ugly adult
with drinks, drugs, smokes
and wines and women
with his morals lost
doesn't turn up
an Idiotic brat......
that his innocence
be not lost
in the world of unsettling plots.

I WANT TO TOUCH THE SEA

I want to touch
the bottom of Ocean
it was my passion
from the day i was fashioned
to softly caress the heart
of the melting waters
to lie upon sea hugged
by little drops of moisture
all around they cling to me
and soak me with wetness
the sponging humid eyes
and glassy looks of tears
the massaging liquidity
yes, i want to sink
deep into the ocean
where lovely corals don't touch
and aquatic lives don't pinch
i love them, yet,
now when i am in love
with the depths
in my watery bed
no compromising heads
don't poke into my love nest
i have the prettiest conquest
with closed eyes
and caved mind
with flame of life aglow
within the soul
here i am, sinking
sinking not sin-king
neither s-inking
but simply I wish

the water and I
be no more two bodies
but hug into and form into
one eternal surrender
into one fusion
with me no mention
just into invisible Abstract Nouns
i want to disseminate
just to disappear into nothing..

AN OSCAR FOR INDIA

We beg
please your attention
we are all slum dogs
wagging for your intentions

yes, we lick your toes
with no remorse
we kiss your paths
thorns don't prick us sharp

Our culture we sell
for your money please
and all our music we fill
with your choices with ease

Our traditions to waste
it is only history to taste
we film for white man's whims
import adultery to chase his aims

Our brides we parade
with whiteness betrayed
for men of money to trade
and semen her along with funds

We Indians shall bow
to any man who shows
coffers of coins in gold
our need is money old or sold

Purity is not in our search
we need to mix to remix

and fix and refix to six
just for dollars we lie and lisp.

Our lady we in nude
angles adjust for your brood
degrees of beauty you decide
just give us money -us slum dogs.

Our music like our mother
we feel just is old and weary
she doesn't dress to party
knows not what is modernity

we in adult adultery believe
to usher in brand new life
and language to this century
pregnant India with foreign luxury

Your Oscars are to our taste
we shall kill any domestic to feast
to be known, to be famous
we shall rejoice in compromise

Thanks for the Oscars
we slum dogs are happy
thanks for the golden idols
our streets neat with nappies.

THE INFANT BEGGAR

Soaked to full
my heart and body
shivering with cold
I saw the child
the little street child
the infant beggar
on the cold pavement
licking at the torn leaf
of a wasted banyan tree
a little food and few tit bits
sticking on to the adhesive plate
poor thing hunger biting its walls
acidic profusion doing its calls
I was sad, that the rain has wet me
I am sadder still that the little brain
is drained for just a little food.......

RAINBOW AT END OF LIFE

Incessant rains
flooded my life
day in and day out
they wept into my life

Creeping into every nook and corner
of every joy they wiped me dear

All day passed into nothing
into dark pits I fell climbing above ill things
every time I stand, some dirty hearts pull me within
and ugly minds pinch me stretching
I screamed at nothings and climbed still to something.
Yet, life was done, so I thought, my dusk nearing.

Sun about to set slowly smiled peeping
I could see the tear drops glistening
Across the heart strings intriguing
some alien hand drew a rainbow colourful
combined with past, present and future in full
Before I sank to ground, I just fluttered open my lull

Ahoy! That was the Rainbow of life, I bowed in Awe.

GOD SEES MY TEARS

I kneel down and weep
but I am not sad at all
deep within something caresses me
I want to cry without any sorrow steep

Pain peeps in body and pins me down
As I lay down pinched all over by aging gowns
somebody whispers unto my heart and sings a song
Song I have never heard, with nectar of life throng.

I pray, holding my hands in gratitude
I owe to all the unknowns in my life
and as I falter at each and every step
some unknown hand it extends from behind

Tears roll down flooding my breasts
I am touched both at heart and mind
my pain someone slowly scrubs, with hands of satin
I cry and clap with joy and sadness moves to silent strains

Gods are moving around on earth as men
when I zoomed my vision I did see them one by one
with heart disillusioned I was dying all these days
till one by one they tumbled down from heaven
like boys from the tops of haystack heaps.

Editor's Note :- Hemangi Sharma (Lalitha) wrote this on July 13, 2015 when
she was most like in her home town Jammu. These was two weeks before
she met me in person for the first time. She said this was the time when she
was first able to overcome the grief of her past life.

LORD CAME IN A DREAM

Just when I slept
a music floated
I thought it a dream
and slept away
but no, it was the call of heavens
but I slept away
and when I awoke
my life's labour I missed
Just when I slept
the painting crept
I took it for a dream
and slept away
yet it was my life drawing
and sobbing I woke up
in the morning, I lost it so close
just when i stood
at the door, half closing
you came, oh lord
you came in the form of a beggar
to give me your holy alms
I closed the door and said no
no more coins to begging ones
I beg you mercy
mercy to cling unto you
you asked me to be merciful
to learn the art of mercy
I asked for some love
u asked me to love, i wished to sing
you told me to enjoy the songs
things have to come from within
how can i ask without doing.

ENCHANTING MANTRA

When I sat upon the couch
a little wonder fondled my breast
silently it said, come on let us rest
forsake all worries, forgo all thoughts
it is time to sleep the mind of furrows
I closed my eyes
blinded my vision from the moving world
started gliding down the world of leisures
I danced upon my breath
it went up and down
and beat upon my heart
wooing it to pump
I was in the wilds
in the forest of greens and birds
my ears could hear music of divine
silently messages clear I could view
distant hearts like dark old caves
lit with candles glowed and showed up
their murmurings and affections for me
I was in the lap of too many world
stroked with visions of saints of heavens
I am not drunken neither drugged
here am I in my little hut
with closed eyes and trembling life
deeply immersed in the vibrant cosmic
Into the (en) chanting mantras I swim.

LANTERN IN THE STORM

Like a lantern in storm
my life's lamp flickers
left and right I lean against
life and death
equally cheers me ahead
am I alive
I am also dead
dreams appear live
life appears dreamy
serious matters casually glance by
but silly things I keenly watch
my heart quivers
emotions tremble
who am I? my mind is zero
I am nearly nothing
thoughts are kidding
pulling my legs
decisions like waves
come and go
squeezing my energies
as they retreat;
chillness surrounds me
at times loneliness freezes me
the dead and unborn companies me
like the lamp in the dark
molten gold drops by
I am waxing like the moon
waning with fantasies
in the tide of life
i am sitting upon paper boat
untied and wild
my life swims to distant islands

starry delights cushion my nights
sundry fish schools stir my lights
I am too empty to live
too silly to survive
my passions like soap bubbles
burst into empty airs
as I fly to catch their hairs

I am the lantern in the storm
sprinkling light
to a few flies
who throb around
in the cold killing night
they just touch upon my glass
and giggle in delight
they kiss my dying flicker
and hug my brooding hotness
happy are they, know not my end nears
that my life half spent, has little to offer
that this lantern is just a spark about to blower.

COME KISS ME

When I shut my eyes
and writhe in pain
as my heart heaves to leave
Oh my love, come to my side
gently kiss me without pride
for deep do I sink into the slide
Love me to wipe my tears
lessen the pain of my years
aged, as I reflect still
you, your voice and your smiles
slowly fondle my bruises
I wonder if you were among the stars
that send messages at silent darks
when the world is asleep
as I silently weep
I do wonder if you were there
The hours of joy we beguiled
the hearts of humour we pried
What is love? Do lovers love
or do they mate with missions intend
Lustless love is dusted free
in thy eyes gems sparkle
portrayals of past miracles

Love is the Rhythm
that links births and rebirths
fluting my frail body to sing
forget the agonies of strings
its the aroma of fertility
perfume of positive energy
the kiss of God on hungry hearts.

SOAK ME IN LOVE RAIN

My heart
I pen
as my ink bleeds
when my life seeds
sown in the wild
did not sprout
and borne out weeds
I verse with my blood
in touch with none
when i feel sad and sunken
to ease my pain
of loneliness and strain
beauty of nature I see
but nature of beauty I cant be
game of love I do play
but to love the game i cant stay
my heart is only a pump
yet, as i lie it silently hums
melodies of life and moans
it aches with the world of flies
flies that die when you live
and show your life beguiles
i cry for each of the roadside whores
who have lost their lovely stores
for the sake of hunger and hood
they who lost the spice of motherhood
the fallen blooms in their early youth
little do they know life is their own truth
when you lie, my heart sinks
and hurt am I losing my links
good and bad are in the eyes
yet empty lives are serious lies

my lines are streams
from soul's dreams
i unfold one by one
just to tease my brain
love dies when senses fail
senses fail as old age sails
shall we exchange our hearts
for brains of wisdom of carts
young hearts for old brains prudent
soak me, oh soak me in love
with melody rained.

MY HEART MIRRORS THE PAST

One by one
as hands of someone
light the life lamp
in the heavens ramp
my heart mirrors
days of my past
and hours of family prayers
lost in empty words

Dusk signals birds
now go to nest
squirrels to their holes
to fatigue's rest
and maids to huts retreat
for hot porridge treat
darkness then spells
a new world of meet
where life begins anew
and old dispels.

MY BLEEDING HEART

Bleeds red
the hole in my heart;
blue roses wreathed
pain stabs my heart

I weep at the broken twig
bleating calf
fallen leaf
and the fur-less chick

I sob at the motherless babes
the blind kid miserable
the sinking huts
and struggling poverty

my heart bleeds
when heartless hearts
sans kindness bake
the poor emotions
of conscientious souls

Is there a god?
does he ever see
when the poor weep
and the rich sleep
Is he awake?
to wipe the tears
and wake up the others.

BEAUTY IN PAIN OF LIFE

Pain
who coined it?
is it beautiful
or ugly?
why no word could partner it?
You could not marry pain to joy
pain is always panting in the pan
fried with self imposed aches and agonies
scanning self introspection, self torture, self punishments
the list of masters controlling the mind

Pained
at the fall of a bud
at the call of the cuckoo
at the look of a pet dog
which has not company
pained at the eyes of deprivation
the images of loneliness
cruelty, perverted savagery, hypocrisy, dirty bestiality
what is pain which rules my heart and yours too.

Pain is the suffering of faith
but faith - who are you?
faith is the tube of connectivity
between foetus and the mother's blood
supplying life and food to baby life
faith in love and wellbeing of lives
expectation of reciprocation of feelings
when faith is cut or is about to be cut
the dying child of life suffers
it withers and is wiped out

Pain is just a sign of annihilation
of the urge to live, to be happy, to enjoy
it cuts off the reason for your existence
why live, why exist in this maddening world
if there are no loving and lovable creatures
if only money speaks, why selfishly breathe
you, your family, your pride, ego, ends and needs
trample, crush, rape, plunder all other innocence
if life is without giggles and laughters
without smiles or sparkles of love
without compassion or kindness
why breathe to just eat and mate
why breathe to kill your brethren

Paining is raining of sadness perennially
when as humans we expect nothing
but minimum decencies, basic courtesies
simple warmth, willingness to co-exist
just do not steal, do not pollute my garden
do not pluck my flowers, do not thorn my heart
with your vampish attacks on life
may every beauty of being thrive
do not bury the new born
with your sarcastic tribe.

A TEAR FELL ON RAINBOW

From the azure blue skies
I saw a tear falling down

It fell on a rainbow

I flew up to the rainbow
to taste the tear
that fell from your beautiful eyes

I just remembered
how I lifted you up
in my arms
to see the rainbow
in glowing colors

Then you listened to the songbirds
and became a song

You smiled then
the joy on your lips
warmth in your eyes
I shall never forget in my life

God's garden must be beautiful
God is grateful to me now
that He has you in His garden

A GREAT SOUL PASSES

It was on its way
the soul of divine says
it just visited the earth
and world of humans it met
to tell them of faith and comets
that brings luck and fortune
for those who strive to find

Dreams are not sleep films
but films that sleep don't dream
what a beauty, what a philosophy
what inspiration to hard work and sweat
Wings of fire, fire with wings
call him Missile man with heart of gold
man who asked us to fly above clouds
to avoid rains that dampens our hopes.

Modest yet multi-millionaire of faith
every quote smells of the heart inside the man
by reading his lines, you can identify the man
the poor born who made us rich
from earth to sky, he missiled by
conquered hearts with kindred smiles
Once in a life time, the King walks us by
Greatness is not a shop brand
this he made us understand
born simple and humble he showed us
how to kite our desires and dreams
the soul was whisked away
when mortal body on its stage beamed
What an escape job the great soul did
Not on bed, nor on hospital's lounges

When intellect was braining to millions
when the eyes twinkled with urge
to share the wisdom conquered
down the destiny's time out
like a vision of God
he landed his vehicle to heavens
What an Avatar he was
Son of his beloved Mother
who loved his brethren
and bread less borns.

Vision were his eyes
Watch were his legs
Epitome of discipline
Monument of modesty and simplicity
A man who left us without leaving

A Purush who enriched us with Artha.

Editor's Note :- This was the last poem written by Hemangi Sharma as "Lalitha Iyer" while her relationship with me was active. It was written on July 28, 2015 – the day after President Abdul Kalam passed away. Hemangi Sharma spent almost that entire day with me. We discussed Dr APJ Kalam's life and works in detail.

Purush :- Male or Man (as against Stree – Woman). Also Purusha stands for the Universal Being in Vedic texts.

Artha :- One of the four goals of life – accumulation of wealth through righteous means (other three being Dharma, Kama and Moksha)

Wings of Fire :- Title of Dr Kalam's autobiography – symbolising the Agni missile. Also symbolises Dva Suparna (Two Birds of Great Wings - glorified in Rig Veda).

EPILOGUE

HEMANGI SHARMA

AS LALITHA IYER

I AM NOT FAKE

My dear poet friend
It is not a fake ID
Only my pseudonym
And I am not theoretical poet
I am a class one English poet
Though an unconventional poet
And an off the cuff instant poet
Name and fame I do not care
I am already published
In many languages
In many formats

Shakespeare was not my dear
A follower like you poor poet
He was a poem in flow
You must have your own DNA
To become a poet of substance
I have been to a poetry academy
Where they once stripped me nude
And now my poems alone they salute

HEMANGI SHARMA

AS SMT LALITHA IYER

It was sometime in the year 2007 when I first noticed certain unusual activities in the internet during my browsing of spiritual topics. Social media posts by different persons with different IDs had the same underlying pattern and digital footprint. When I tried to follow some of these posts, I started receiving similar posts in my e-mail ID as spam messages. Although I found it quite baffling, I thought it could be just a coincidence.

In 2009 a woman started stacking me online and also over phone. I received a series of calls from a woman claiming to be Swapna from Bangalore. Sometimes the woman told me that she was working as an executive at Google India office, while at other times she said she was working at Facebook. The woman started calling me from different phone numbers, each time giving a different name such as Swapna, Jyoti, Kiran, Savita etc. It was quite obvious that it was the same woman, since the voice, accent, style and intonation was the same. It was also obvious that she was stalking me for an ulterior motive, since a Google or Facebook executive would have little to do with someone like me who had hardly any presence on social media.

During the years 2011 and 2012 there was a marked reduction in the stalking activity of this woman. So I had largely forgotten aouut those spam calls and messages. But then suddenly in September 2013 a woman named Chitrangdha K Ganesh sent me a message on Poemhunter website. The title of her message read "I am bowled over by your poetic skills". It was very perplexing. I

In August 2013 I had exposed certain fraudulent activities in the online Poemhunter Poetry Competition, in which I was a participant. I found that out of the 100 poems reaching the final, 37 appeared to be the works of same person. The poems showed exquisite craftsmanship and were on wide ranging topics. But all these 37 poems had a typical signature style. Many of these poems had been submitted by poets with similar names such as Prem Kumar, Prem Jyot, Prem123 etc. I had lodged a written complaint with Poemhunter.com website regarding such fraud, but received no response.

When I received the mail from Chitrangdha initially I thought as if the sender had some divine connection with me. But immediately I remembered the Poemhunter fraud, and thought this woman could be connected with that episode. Either the woman herself was the fraudster, or maybe some Poemhunter staff investigating the fraud. So I was wary of disclosing any details about me to this woman.

Although initially I avoided the woman, she kept on sending me her e-mail IDs and mobile numbers, requesting me to share my contact details. Although I was wary of the woman, finally curiosity got the better of me. I did some online chatting with the woman on Poemhunter platform. She introduced herself to me as a freelance worker in the field of advertisement and tourism. However after some time she started contradicting her own statements. Sometimes she said she was a researcher, a student, and IT professional or even a journalist. Sometimes she said she was married, and sometimes unmarried. Sometimes she said she was 39 years old, and at other times 33 or 43.

In April-May 2014 "Chitrangdha" obtained from me my mobile number and called me. In her very first call she told me about her life-long desire to study the Rg Veda and Qu'ran. She also told me that one day she would like to come to my house to study the Veda and Qu'ran with me. I found it quite surprising. Because ever since my childhood I had an unusual interest in the scriptures, and I had particular fascination for the rhythmic mantras of Rg Veda and Sama Veda as well as for the melodious Ayats of Quran as rendered by the Muezzins in mosques.

I developed a very intimate online relationship with this Chitrangdha. She was the first person with whom I had any personal chats online. She exchanged hundreds of messages with me via Facebook, WhatsApp, Poemhunter, SMS and other media. Sometimes she would call me up to ten times in a day. Often she told me that it was her life-long desire to come to my house and spend the rest of her life with me. I found t very strange. I suspected of a past life connection with her.

On June 5, 2015 Chitrangdha revealed to me that her actual name was Hemangi Sharma, and that she was a student at National Institute of Rural Development, Hyderabad. She also admitted that she had been trolling me since 2009 under a series of fake IDs. She said she came to know about me from a person named Basant Kumar Rath, a senior police officer posted in Jammu. This Basant Rath was my childhood friend and had studied with me in the same class up to university level. Hemangi Sharma aka Chitrangdha had been born and brought up in Jammu before she moved to Bangalore and Hyderabad for job.

In July 2015 I met Hemangi Sharma at her office in Hyderabad. She had invited me to participate in the annual convocation ceremony of her institute. She had booked a room for me in her office guest house. I spent two days with her. During those two days she shared with me her life story. She also discussed the hidden secrets of various world scriptures including the Bible and the Qu'ran. The religious philosophies that Hemangi Sharma discussed with me are the same that Antony Theodore has described in detail in his Christian poems.

When I met Hemangi Sharma in person she did not admit that she was Antony Theodore. But she admitted that she had hundreds of fake IDs. She showed me how she had created multiple Ids by using different mobile phones and SIM cards. But when I asked her to open Chitrangdha's e-mail, she said she had forgotten Chitra's password. When I asked her why she had opened so many fake IDs, she said that she had worked as a marketing executive at Google and Facebook, and that sending spam advertisements to unsuspecting customers was part of her lucrative corporate job. She also said that she had got fed up with that kind of artificial and unethical job, and therefore she had quit the job to pursue a career in rural development.

Initially Hemangi Sharma had shared with me those IDs through whch she had been sending spam mails. But after I came back from Hyderabad, Hemangi Sharma gradually revealed to me her other IDs under which she had posted thousands of poems online. Then only I realised Hemangi Sharma's true stature as a world class poet. I was surprised that she had not published even a single poem under her own name. All her poems had been published under hundreds of pseudonyms. After introducing me to her poetry, Hemangi Sharma deactivated her original e-mail IDs. So I was forced to correspond with her via her fake IDs. She discussed her poetry with me in great detail over thousands of messages exchanged through such fake IDs. And then one fine day she deleted all her messages to me. That left me with no evidence that she had indeed discussed her poetry with me. However I managed to save a few of those messages as proof of her correspondence with me.

Hemangi Sharma has uploaded thousands of her poems in different languages under hundreds of fake IDs. She is a multi-linguist with scholarly understanding of all major world religions. One fails to understand why a spiritual person like her would use so many fake IDs, which is a criminal offence. But then strange are the ways of the devotees of God.

When Hemangi Sharma first started corresponding with me, I immediately knew that she was the person behind the hundreds of fake IDs under which she had uploaded her poems. However she admitted to it much later, only after I relentlessly pursued her to know the truth. She has the talent and creativity to write spontaneously in thousands of different styles. But there were certain underlying patterns in all her works. The most common element in her writings is her use of small "i" to denote the first person singular. She purportedly did so to underplay the individual ego in the creative process. But there is still no plausible explanation for the use of thousands of fake IDs. She could have adopted a single pseudonym to mask her identity, but she chose to have thousands. I believe that she wrote under fake IDs to completely dissociate her ego from the creative process. I myself had resorted to such a technique during my student days. I found that the poems I had written under pseudonyms were qualitatively much better than those published under my real name.

Another underlying pattern in Hemangi Sharma's writings is her utter disregard for the conventional rules of grammar. Among all her online avatars, I found Dr Tony Brahmin (Antony Theodore) as comparatively the most conventional one in terms of style. Lalitha Iyer was a mixture of conventional style and unconventional word play. However certain freedom in use of language can also be seen in Antony's poems.

Yet another frequent feature in Hemangi Sharma's writings is the use of abbreviations, colloquial expressions and liberal use of nouns as verbs and adjectives. For instance she would write "RV Lovers" instead of "Are We in Love". You is abbreviated to "u" in most of her writings. Instead of "more childish", she will simply write "childer". For instance, in one of her letters to me, she wrote "love makes heart become childer". Even mobile SMS texts such as Gn and Tc (goodnight, take care etc) frequently appear in her poems. She also uses past, present and future tenses in the same poem as part of the same dialogue between protagonists. This reflects her belief that time is an illusion, and that earthly concept of time does not exist at all in the realm of God consciousness.

What makes her art so special is that she makes such unusual expressions quite spontaneously. The reader hardly suspects that she is deliberately doing so. Classical English expressions gladly coexist with ultra-modern sms texts.

In addition to "Antony", Hemangi Sharma has also adopted other interesting pseudonyms such as Lalitha Iyer, Dev Anand, Poet Poet, Sun Princess, April Pearl and a host of other IDs. She has used both male and female names, as well as names from different languages. She has used Hindu names, Christian names and Muslim names. Maybe she did so to identify herself with all humanity irrespective of artificial barriers created by gender, race, caste, language and religion.

But still she could have managed to do all this with 30 or 40 IDs. I really don't know what could have been Hemangi Sharma's real intention in adopting hundreds and thousands of fake IDs. Any discerning reader would have noticed the underlying pattern in the poems written under different IDs. But perhaps nobody pointed it out before I did so. I was the only person who lodged a written complaint regarding her fake IDs. Perhaps Hemangi

Sharma deliberately did so with the expectation that someday someone would find out her real identity. Perhaps it was God's design that I would become that person. Or maybe it was Hemangi Sharma's own design – who knows?

Hemangi Sharma had frequently expressed to me her desire to open a school for underprivileged children, and also to adopt a baby girl with my financial support. She wanted to have an unconventional school, which would be completely free from the curriculum of rote learning. She told me that she wanted me as the Mentor of her "school". I do not know what exactly was in my mind. I asked her to explain to me her idea of "mentor". But she was evasive in her answers. However, from the very beginning of her interactions with me she clearly told me about her disapproval of abortion of foetuses. Protection of children and their precious childhood was her topmost priority, and it took up bulk of her conversations with me. She said she had left her lucrative corporate job to take up the study of rural development solely for the purpose of empowering vulnerable women and underprivileged children.

Lalitha Iyer's early poems are full of sadness and disgust at the unjust society full of hypocrisy. But her later poems are full of joy and optimism. There is a distinct difference in the style and treatment in her poems before she contacted me and after that. Hemangi Sharma stopped writing under the ID of Lalitha Iyer after meeting me in person. Thereafter she exchanged with me thousands of messages, but wrote no new poems as Lalitha. In one of her messages Lalitha had told me that she was going to kill herself. At that time I did not understand what she meant. But now I understand that she meant Lalitha would not write any more poem. After meeting me Hemangi Sharma completely dedicated herself to social work, and wrote only some religious poems under the name "Antony".

But from my extensive discussions with her I clearly understood that whenever she was talking about sadness she was not referring to her own personal grief, but the pain of seeing human beings forgetful of God.

Tapan Kumar Pradhan

9 788194 579731